white hot

white hot

tricia guild
cool colors for modern living

photographs by james merrell

text by elspeth thompson with tricia guild

Clarkson Potter/Publishers
New York

for lisa with more than love

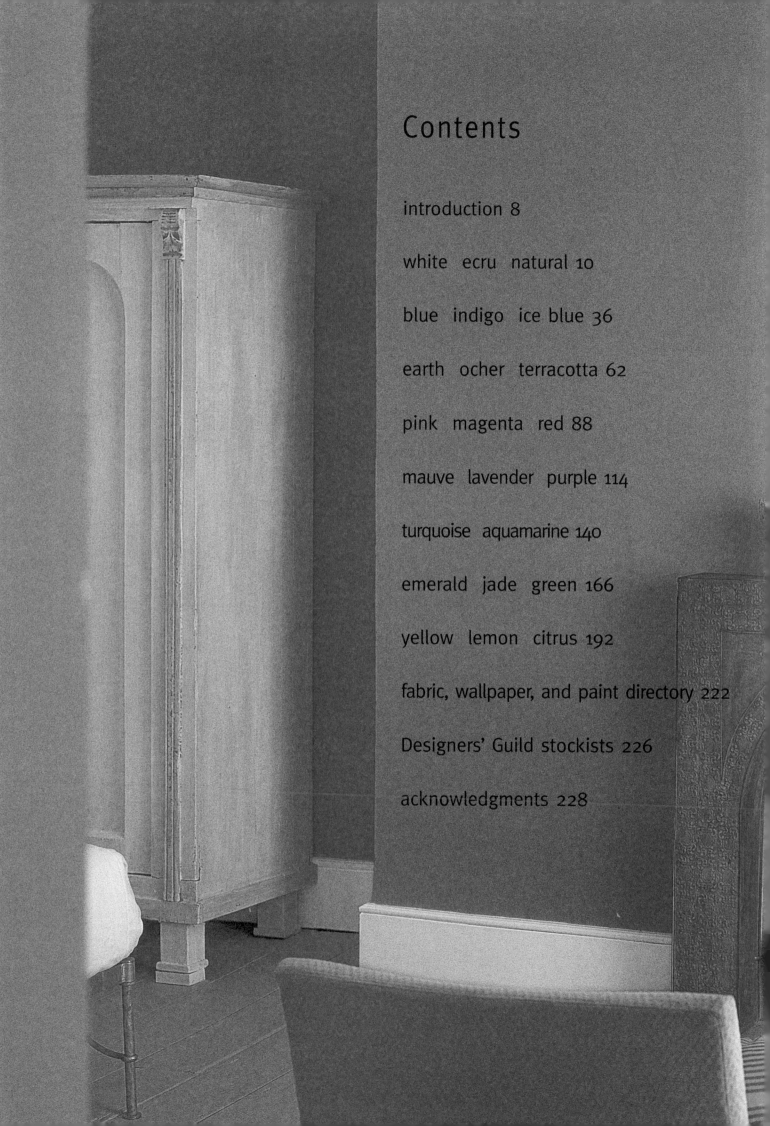

Contents

introduction

There has always been a constant presence in my mind of a particular shade of blue, nearly mauve, which is both fragile and intense, provoking a vibrant energy within me. One of the major joys of my work has been my constant contact with color, a vast arena in which I am always searching for a deeper awareness of the qualities of different colors and what they bring to the individual—working with shades, texture, light, pattern, and shape, exploring color to its fullest depth and then exploring again, looking for a balance of color that evolves until something inside clicks into place.

My response to color has always been intensely personal and emotional. Color theory and scientific explanations are not my way of searching—I prefer intuitive responses. Nor do I take any notice of the old-fashioned so-called "rules." We're told that pinks and orange clash; but you only have to imagine the vibrancy of bougainvillea and orange trees in an Italian garden, or the singing stripes and borders of Indian women's saris, to know that may not be so. I look to nature for inspiration, to the uninhibited spontaneity of other cultures experienced on travels abroad, and to the work and wisdom of artists.

An understanding of color, in my view, is acquired through observing and allowing the responses to blossom. For colors are not constants. They are subtle chameleons, taking on the character of the shapes, spaces, and objects they occupy. Light affects our response to color on both aesthetic and emotional levels. The same color on a sunny wall will look very different under artificial light. The quality of sunshine itself varies around the world. The other vital influence on mood is texture. Think of the difference in response to a deep pink velvet and a pink shiny car; the soft fragrant green of a leaf and the rustling glamour of silk of the same color.

When decorating our houses we make deliberate choices about what colors to use where. But all the time, every day, we are making decisions based unconsciously on color—the clothes we put on, the vegetables we choose in the supermarket. We can learn much about our innate sense of color by becoming more aware of these spontaneous responses. It is through a combination of instinct and contemplation that one arrives at an individual sense of color. This sense of color can change or be renewed. After many years of using bright, saturated color, I have recently moved toward a calmer, quieter, more harmonious use of color which seems in tune with how I live now. The balance has changed. I always used more white and natural colors than people may have supposed, but whereas white was previously a "silent partner" working alongside the brighter colors, it has now moved to center stage.

My favorite colors now include slate-gray, a rich, purply grape, lavender, chartreuse, and aqua. I am attracted to the farthest extremes of the color groups: blue just before it becomes mauve and green when it's neither blue nor green. Every color can be taken down to its flattest neutral "roots": gray-blue, olive-green, peat, or mustard-yellow. These, together with accents of the brighter colors, have given rise to a new way of working with color.

We have grouped colors together loosely, reflecting their emotional as well as aesthetic qualities. For instance, different shades of orange might be found in both the "earth colors" chapter and the one introducing pinks and reds. Photographs of my own homes in London and Italy, and other interesting spaces, show how different amounts of colors, used with white and naturals, can completely transform a room. Our houses have been changed, but sometimes just by tweaking the balance rather than repainting every wall. By taking up rugs to expose pale wood floors, reupholstering a sofa in a cooler shade, and changing the cushions and curtains, one can create a totally new atmosphere. A dilution of color brings an intense awareness of texture—the added richness of different layers of silk, linen, cotton, wood, metal, glass, wool, or washed chenille. Pattern and geometry take on a new potency.

More than in my other books, I want to illustrate how I work; to convey the process by which a spontaneous combination of green and lilac, glimpsed on a house in India, can become the inspiration for an interior back home. A passionate response—to a flower just opening, the peeling paint on a building, or the bathing-suit of a young woman in a vacation photo—can thus be integrated into the space in which you live. This cannot help but bring more passion, beauty, and individuality into all our lives.

Tricia Guild

white

blanc

bianco

ホワイト

weiß

white

blanc

bianco

ホワイト

weiß

white

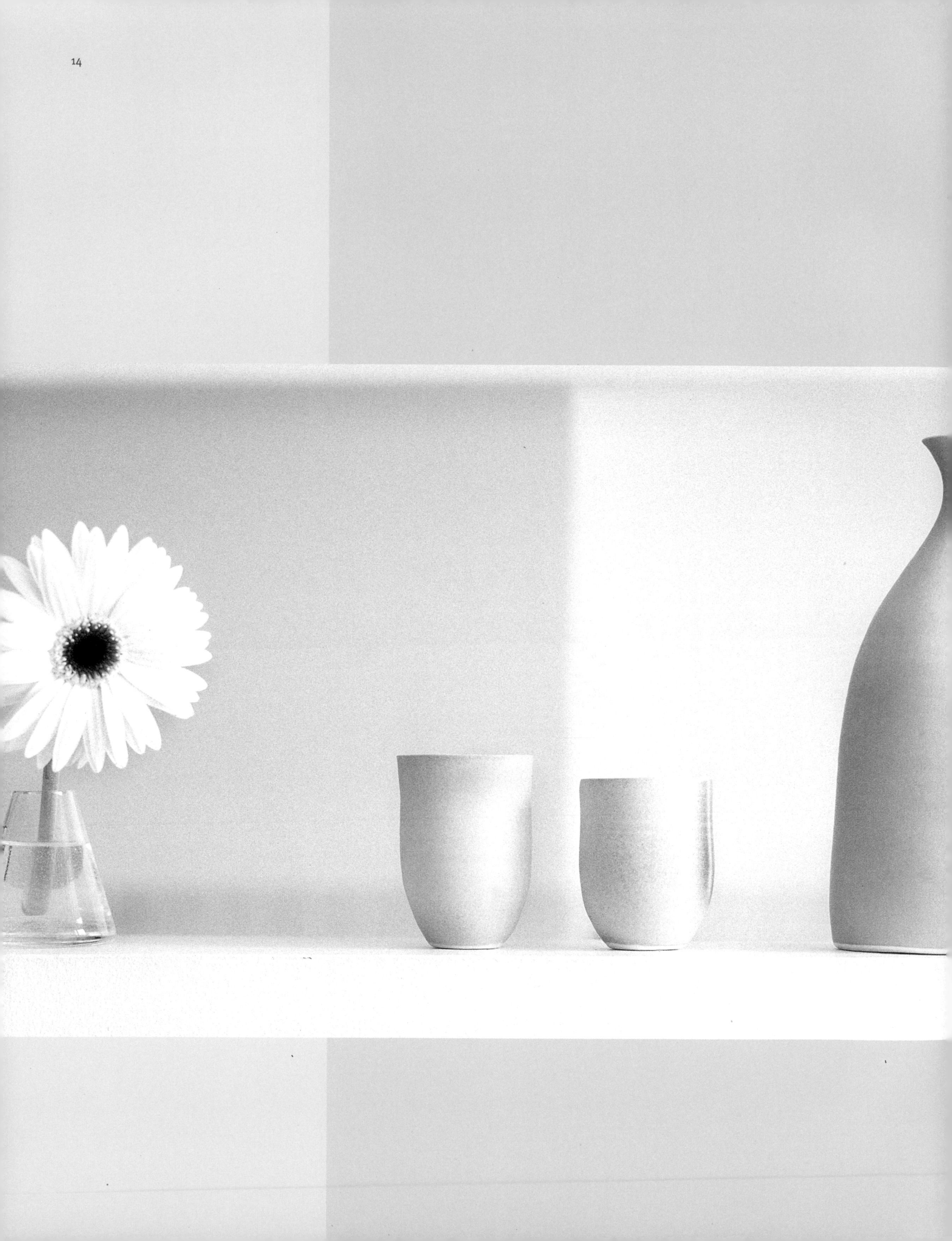

White is a mystery. Scientists tell us it is not a color at all, but represents white light in which all colors are blended. Of all the shades to work with, pure white is the most susceptible to changes of light and shade. Much of what we call white is, in fact, tinged with other colors.

Snow is white. Or is it? Look at a Whistler snow scene and see how many different colors the artist has chosen to depict the white of the snow. There will be purple in the shadows, pale blue in the light of the sun, with all the subtlest shades of blue-gray, mauve, pink, cream, and even yellow in between. There may not be any pure white at all—that bright splash reflecting the strongest glare of sunshine may appear white, but place a piece of white paper in front and it looks pale green.

Milk is white, but compared with pure white it has a bluish cast, as does cheap white latex flat paint. Eggshells have a creamy tinge; bone is yellowish; most white flowers are shot with palest green, especially in bud. Picture a bed covered in crumpled linen sheets as the pinkish dawn light penetrates the patterns of the folds; then in the noonday sun; in electric light; in golden candlelight. With every moment, white is different; it takes on other hues and sheds them as time passes.

White is a powerful color. Besides changing with the light, it reflects it, transforming other colors around it. When you awake after an overnight snowfall, the whole room looks different. When juxtaposed with white or off-white, colors can be seen in their purest intensity.

minimalism with soul: planes of pure white and pale textures

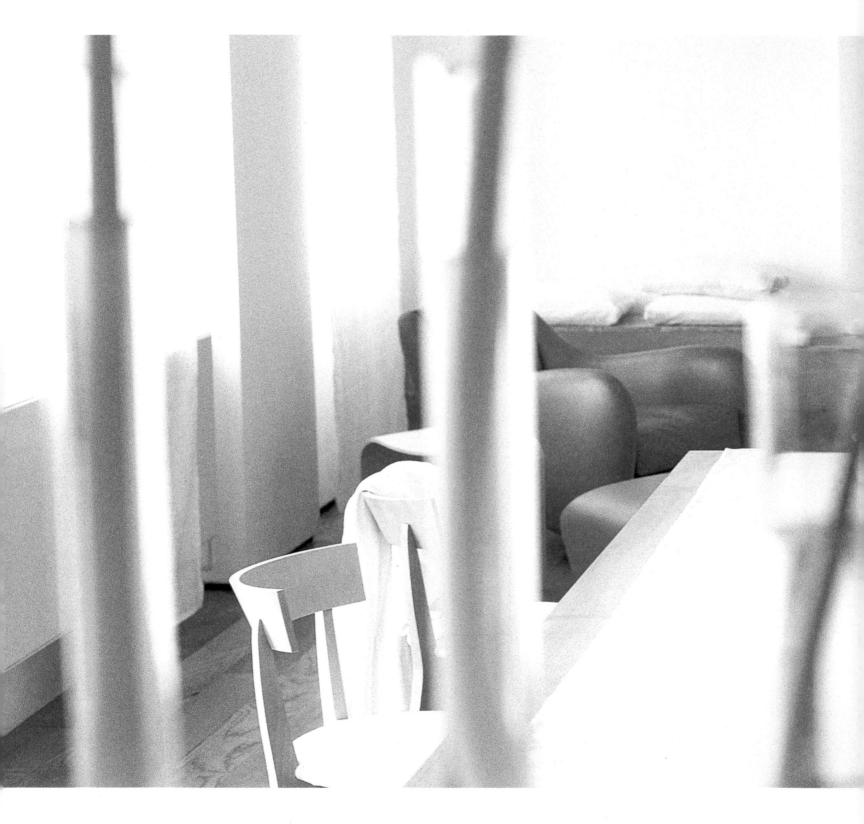

In this modern house, white paint and a variety of pale textures have created an oasis of calm in the heart of the city. Pure white paint is the perfect foil for

the calm but graphic style of the architecture—at different times of the day the vertical and horizontal planes and the slightly slanted ceilings appear grayish,

pale mauve, warm cream, or searing clear white, illustrating the subtle richness of this color. But this is no stark minimalism: soft textures and variations in

color abound. White linen with drawn threadwork hangs at the windows, softening the cityscape below, while a runner of cream linen skims the length of a

pale wood table. Paler natural tones, from the wood of floors and furniture to the warmth of leather cushions, create a visual and tactile feast.

White walls, ash floors, pale gray tiles, and concrete fireplaces are the backdrop for an interplay of off-white materials and textures—pale oak furniture, white linen, the bluish cast of porcelain, the palest gray glaze of Japanese stoneware. Natural whites and off-whites soften what might otherwise appear to be a slightly sterile space—white gerberas, the milky greens of calla lilies.

The impression of almost monastic simplicity belies a luxurious use of texture. In the bedroom, a plain wooden bed and small sunken

square windows are countered by crisp linen sheets and covers and by cushions of silk and soft washed chenille velvet, demonstrating a

sensuous awareness of light and the feel of fabric. Texture takes on a new significance when working with white, cream and naturals.

Morning light on Lake Pichola, India

photograph: Tricia Guild

With its chameleon qualities, white is a fascinating color in interior spaces. In a room that has good natural light, one could sit back and let the day-long changes in sun and shadow work their magic on white walls, floor, and fabrics, and accentuate the changes with a vase of bright flowers, a large abstract painting, or a richly woven carpet.

But white also lends itself to experiments with texture. Subtle changes in light make us minutely aware of surface detail: the softness of washed cotton, the iridescence of white silk, the creamy deep pile of sheepskin. The play of different textures against one another appeals to more senses than sight alone: consider the cool glamour of white marble, the satisfying simplicity of slip-glazed plates piled with chalky-rinded cheese; the way hands instinctively reach out to a closet full of fluffy white towels.

Even if white and off-white are the only colors used, the effects will be endlessly enriching. Exploit all the variations. Each nuance of white will lead you toward different areas of color—to cream, oatmeal shades, mushroom, dove-gray, and ecru—each of which has its own qualities. The effects can be surprising. While naturals don't exactly clash, great care is needed when mixing them. Yellowish naturals don't always sit well next to grayish tones; too many different shades of cream create a cloying, claustrophobic atmosphere. The paler shades of wood, such as ash, beech, and bleached wood, act as colors in their own right in this group, so consider the tonal qualities they bring with them.

When working with the whole spectrum of colors, you should always use white and its other natural counterparts as a balancing presence—as an anchor for moments of intensity. If one or two walls are treated with bright color, leave the others and the ceiling white and the floors pale wood. White gives other colors room to breathe, to stop competing, to be themselves.

natural textures and cool white complement one another in natural light

Natural daylight brings out the fine variations of texture among natural materials such as wood, linen, stone, rope, paper, cotton, raw plaster, metal.

Tones of ecru, pale stone, and straw-like string: these are the colors at the lighter end of the natural palette, and they work well with white and

almost all other colors. Against this cool neutral ground, splashes of color—a mauve cushion, the brushwork of an abstract painting—can sing out in

contrast. In a room such as this, which has skylights open to changing cloud patterns and doors that open wide to the outside, the colors of nature

are also brought into play: the green of the garden is glimpsed in the background, the tones and textures further enriched by the metal mesh screen

on the balcony. Glass reflects color and takes on the tones of the objects around it; aluminum works here as a neutral, cool silver-gray.

blue shadows and white linen—a contemporary combination

Pure white can look blue in certain lights, and some whites have a bluish cast; play on this ambiguity by using white and pale powder blues in a cool modern bedroom. The classic combination of blue and white is given a contemporary twist by the lack of tonal contrast, using just a few closely related shades, the mixture of pattern and stripes, and floral fabric hung as folding shades at the window, instead of curtains or draperies.

Although a lot of blue has been used here, the preponderance of white and the paleness of the shades create the impression of a mainly white room. The pale naturals in the scheme—the stone floor and light metal furniture—also read as shades of white, while the hand-thrown white vase is like a piece of modern sculpture.

work in progress

pages 16-19

white ecru natural

Light plays a crucial part when working with white and naturals. The same tone on a sunny wall will look very different under artificial light, and morning light is cooler than afternoon light, which glows more golden into evening. It's not just a matter of aesthetics, either—in a room devoid of strong color, our emotions are strongly affected by an absence or abundance of natural light. The subtle interplay of light and shadow is what activates the qualities of all the different shades, patterns, and textures in these four different rooms, creating variety and richness within the close range of colors.

Pages 16-19 When the only colors you are using are white and shades of off-white, the other natural materials in a room, such as wood, become colors in their own right. In this loft, the natural warm tones of the oak floor led me toward the warm, creamier shades of off-white— eggshell tones, from pale cream to pinky brown and even palest birds'-egg blue. The differences in texture are subtle, but distinct: different weaves of linen, drawn-threadwork, waffle-patterned velvet chenille inject a sensuous note and prevent the white room from feeling severe or clinical.

Pages 20-23 In this bedroom, we turned to pattern for extra layers of richness and interest. Wide stripes, crewel embroidery, and a small stamped image on the wallpaper work well together within a limited palette of cream, natural linen, and warm beige. A delicate tension is set up between the large expanses of natural hard materials, such as the pale wood floor, and the many intimate details—knotted string embroidery, the cream border on the bedcover, the glass bottles and paper boxes beside the bed.

Pages 26-27/32-33 Through the introduction of small and subtle amounts of pale color, white rooms can veer toward different colors: aqua-green in the bedroom on pages 26-27, and pale powder blue on pages 32-33. White and off-white are still the principal colors used, but the pale colors and small-scale floral or paisley prints create an impression of softness and delicacy which manages never to appear fussy. The cool blue-and-white room has a reflective glass wall behind the bed—using transparent cottons and elusive blue-gray tones accentuates the feeling of translucency in the room. I also like combining warm textures with cool colors—the palest slate-blue chenille works particularly well in this bedroom.   TG

pages 20-23

pages 26-27

pages 32-33

for details of fabrics and paints used in the rooms on these pages see page 222

blue bleu sky cobalt forge

blau indigo marin ciel was

azzurro sapphire azurblå h

blå ice agua cielo ghiacci

zafiro blue bleu sky cobal

me-not blau indigo marin

wasser azzurro sapphire a

hyacinth blå ice agua ciel

ghiaccio kobalt zafiro blue

sky cobalt forget-me-not b

ndigo marin ciel wasser a

sapphire azurblå hyacinth

agua cielo ghiaccio kobalt

indigo

kobalt zaffiro

cobalt forget-me-not

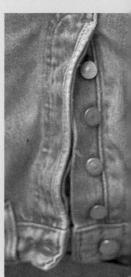

All blues seem to radiate the most extraordinary natural energy. Blue is peaceful, yet it has an expansive quality that feels like freedom.

Perhaps this is because it is the color of the sky. We live our whole lives with different shades of blue above us, from the pale, powdery

blue of a cloudy dawn to the clear azure of a summer sky to deepest, inkiest, midnight blue.

Blue is the color most often chosen by people as their favorite. It is a familiar, comforting color in almost all countries and

cultures. Think of blue-and-white china, blue denim, blue houses in Jodhpur, in India, blue street signs in Paris, blue habits for nuns.

Yet it is also exciting and surprising. Blue runs the arc of the spectrum between aquamarine and mauve, and some of the most

interesting shades are found in those farther reaches—the watery sea-blues that almost cross over into green; the rich purply blues

of agapanthus, delphiniums, and hyacinths. Blue is timeless—always beautiful; never in or out of fashion.

For many centuries in Western art, blue was a precious, holy color; ultramarine was ground from costly lapis lazuli and saved

for the cloak of the Virgin Mary. Since then, artists have found endless inspiration in blue, from Masaccio's Florentine frescos to

Picasso's Blue Period, to that searing, vibrating, bottomless blue that Yves Klein made his own.

Blue is said to be a cool color, but every color has its cool and warm tones. Seek out some of the beautiful warm blues, those

with a lot of red in them that are almost mauve; calm but not cold, these are wonderful colors for bedrooms, living rooms, and studies.

warm blues, cool slate grays, and different textures of white

One wall of this large, light bedroom is a wonderful warm blue, with swirls of pigment laid directly onto raw plaster. The room used to have more

contrasts, but simply by removing the colored rugs to expose the pale wood floors and stepping up the proportion of white, a cooler, more

contemporary look has been created. Former accents of hot pink and lime have been replaced by flat, slate blues and grays, plus a soft lilac which

brings out the mauve in the blue on the wall. White linen curtains filter the sunlight into a soft filmy haze. The brightest color in the room is the

jewel-like bright pink of a tiny painting by Craigie Aitcheson that hangs above the bed.

Shades of white bring a heightened awareness of color, shape, and texture: the white armoire, with traces of blue showing through its chalky matte paint; the plain white bed linen; the scrolling sculptural arms of the chair. Neutrals have to be a whiter shade of pale—too much yellow in the wood floor would throw the whole room off balance.

Glass has a special appearance in blue rooms, its watery qualities accentuated by the surrounding colors. Etched glass doors slide open to the bathroom, their milky whiteness borrowing some of the blue beyond and turning yet another shade. Glass vases and bottles of different shapes and sizes contain single blooms of blue-mauve flowers.

Blues mix well. Most blues look good together, particularly if you contrast the textures: silk and linen; oil paint and velvet; washed denim and cool glass mosaic. When placed next to blues, darker grays and neutrals such as metal can take on an indigo cast, whereas with any other color they would simply read as gray. Glass becomes bluish and watery in its company. Blue in a bathroom is heavenly—a space in which to relax surrounded by the colors of the sea.

Blue is a good ground for other colors. Use it with touches of lime green or with accents of mauve, magenta, or shocking pink. Sometimes just a single flower—a pale mauve scabious or crimson peony—is enough. Blues also look good with neutral colors: turquoise and chocolate-brown, powder-blue and charcoal-gray, navy and ecru are happy combinations. The cooler neutrals work best—think also of the flatter greens, of pale olive and sage. In its flattest, grayest forms, blue itself becomes a neutral, a chalky slate color that looks good with aquas or warm, reddish blues.

White is the natural choice for balancing the use of blue. Blue and white is a fresh and timeless combination: try mixing a variety of different blue-and-white stripes and checks; or use clear, bright blues against whitewashed walls, as they do in Mediterranean lands. Soft gray-blues with white sit well together: in an open, modern space they are cool and neutral, combining well with wood and metal; in more traditional architecture they evoke eighteenth-century Swedish design.

The palace of Fateh Prakash, India

photograph by Tricia Guild

In hotter climates the cooling, calming qualities of blue are particularly welcome in bedrooms, where their natural partners are crisp white sheets and pillowcases. In this large, high-ceilinged room, a rich cobalt blue on the walls complements white paintwork, bed linen, and upholstery, while the warm terracotta of the floor tiles is picked up in accents of pink. A checkered frieze carries a pattern of blue, pink, and lime around the room at baseboard level, along with a deep stripe of dull olive-green. The layers of paint are distressed and textured, suggesting the patina of age. The pink is repeated in an embroidered cushion on the daybed, the greens in the cool stems and budding flowers of white agapanthus in the foreground.

cobalt-blue walls with accents of pink in a Tuscan farmhouse

Subtle accents of pink and green continue in the details of this cobalt blue bedroom. Crewelwork embroidery on an armchair brings all the colors

together: blue, white, clear apple-green, and a wonderful shade between lilac and pink. A throw of the same cotton fabric is laid across the bed, where

silk plaid pillowcases have touches of hotter magenta pink. Greenery brings the spirit of the outside in: the flat gray-green of a hosta leaf, with its

graphic earthy textures, mirrors the olive-green present in the silk plaid draperies and in the line around the base of the walls. This dull, neutral green is a natural foil for bright blue; the combination can be seen over and over again in nature. When the French windows are thrown open, lozenges of light illuminate the different whites and blues of the sheets and cushions, creating new shades of lilac and lavender in the folds and shadows.

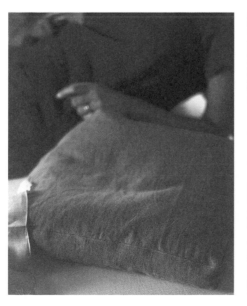

delicate pale slate-blue with stripes and patterns

Delicate use of different patterns and textures of pale blue gives this living room a light, feminine, yet totally modern feel. Pale slate-blues and grays, interspersed with turquoise, peat-brown, and lilac, permeate a neutral ground of pale whitewashed wood floors and paintwork. Stripes—in the celadon pattern on the walls, the cushions, and the upholstery—are coupled with a skillful use of pattern, including rich gold and silver stenciling on the long floral draperies. The clean silhouette of the modern sofa, covered in pale slate-blue chenille, injects a cool, contemporary element into this period architecture; the pale blue plastic chair and metal-legged table continue the light, modern feeling. Even the flowers are fine-textured and feathery, adding another feminine touch to the room.

work in progress

pages 42-45

blue indigo ice blue

Pages 42-45/52-57 The palettes are actually very similar for these two bedrooms in London and Tuscany—warm blues, mauve, lilac, and turquoise to pale blue—but the impression given by the rooms is very different. This is partly due to the different styles of architecture—a modern conversion of a Victorian house in London and a historic rural farmhouse in Italy—and the way the the color used responds to its surroundings. In London, (pages 42-45), the feeling is cool and contemporary, with large expanses of balancing white on walls and furniture. Here, two walls are of a pigment blue just this side of mauve, with organic swirls set directly into the wet plaster. In Italy, (pages 52-57), all the walls are painted a vivid shade of hyacinth—and the use of color is more saturated and intense, with white for the fabric and furniture. The crewelwork chair is the starting point for the decoration of this scheme, with patterns in various shades of blue and a pinkish lilac. But whereas the London room sticks with medium-blues and a washed-out lilac, in Italy I took it farther into deep pink and magenta, in the form of stripes in the bed linen and a silk plaid for throws and pillows. Jewel-bright colors such as this look good used as one or two bright accents in a room; they affect the overall impression of the room very powerfully.

Pages 46-48 The colors of this blue glass-tiled bathroom have been continued into the bedroom beyond, where very rich colors for throws and pillows on the low bed complement the dark wood of the walls. A pink and brown check pulls the whole scheme together; lighter natural shades of taupe, mushroom, and string combine well with the cooler blues.

Pages 58-59 In this living room the blue tones are slightly more green than in the other rooms in this chapter, and there is a slight flatness to pale blues in certain lights which makes them veer toward eau-de-nil. The duck-egg shades mix well together in a variety of stripes and checks and textures, with a pale greenish blue color on the walls. The cooler shades are countered by warm textures, especially the waffle-textured chenille velvets in powder blue and white. The color scheme is anchored by just enough dark chocolate brown—perfect with cool blues and acid greens—to give some strength and backbone to the room.   TG

pages 52-57

pages 46-48

pages 58-59

for details of fabrics and paints used in the rooms on these pages see page 222

earth **chocolat** erde **brown** ocker sto

erracotta bärnsten terra ecru nasturt

wood peat **bois** café amber tie

erde madera copper **schokolade** strin

brandgul earth **chocolat** erde **brown**

stone fuoco terracotta bärnsten terra

nasturtium wood **terre** peat boi

amber **tierra** fire erde madera coppe

string **schokolade** umbra **brandgul** ea

hocolat erde **brown** ocker stone fuoc

erracotta bärnsten terra ecru nasturt

vood peat **bois** café amber tie

rde madera copper **schoko** umbra s

earth chocolat erde brown ocker sto

terracotta bärnsten terra ecru nasturt

wood peat bois café amber tie

erde madera copper schokolade strin

brandgul earth chocolat erde brown

stone fuoco terracotta bärnsten terra

nasturtium wood terre peat boi

amber tierra fire erde madera coppe

string schokolade umbra brandgul ea

chocolat erde brown ocker stone fuo

terracotta bärnsten terra ecru nasturt

wood peat bois café amber tie

erde madera copper schoko umbra s

terracotta ocher earth

Ocher, terracotta, burnt sienna, burnt umber, peat-brown—even the names of colors within this group remind us of their earthy

origins. At one time most colors were ground from earth pigments. When we use these colors, we are conscious of a connection

with the land. Take inspiration from different landscapes—from the pale scorched earth of the Rajasthani desert, the warm red-

brown of plowed furrows, the peeling ocher plaster on the wall of a palazzo in Naples.

There are warm earth colors—fiery oranges, terracottas (literally meaning "fired earth"), copper, warmer naturals, and

browns with more red in them—that make us think of fall, log fires, russet apples, and pumpkins; of auburn hair and the sun on

fallen beech leaves. The cooler side of this palette encompasses dark peaty browns, the rich ebony tones of wenge wood and dark

chocolate-brown ceramics. These colors evoke shape and texture, and the qualities of natural materials that become colors in their

own right, of hand-built clay and curved metal, the grain of wood, the weave of a textile.

Light has a dramatic effect on earth colors, acting almost in partnership with them. Imagine watching the sun rise over a

desert landscape made up of the sandy earth tones. The dawn light is cool, almost mauve, teasing the different colors awake. As

the sun rises, pinkish tones come into play—the pink sand on the hills reflects the warming light onto the delicate air above. At

noon the earth is baked and colors are at their harshest extremes, either blazing blocks of light or dark swathes of shadow. The

golden sun of a late afternoon urges even cooler earth colors aglow; but once the sun has set, even oranges and ochers have the

warmth drained out of them before drifting and disappearing into the gray of dusk.

warm desert colors in a textured setting

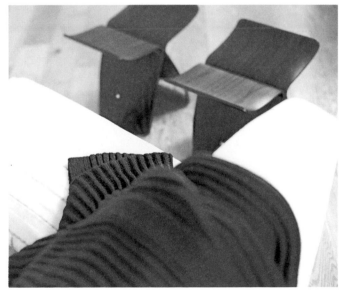

A backdrop of white and naturals has been given added warmth by the introduction of warmer earth tones—the soft pinky browns of terracotta, raw plaster, and sand. More neutral naturals, such as peat-brown and the natural linen muslin that hangs at the windows, can turn either cooler or warmer, depending on what colors accompany them; the atmosphere of the room could be consciously changed with the seasons. Here, the deep recesses of the wooden sofa act almost like another room, furnished in warm terracotta cotton and cushions in peat-brown and pale lime. A richness of tones and textures plays out in the details: chocolate-brown suede, sculptural wax candles, handthrown pots, and the slub in the weave of linen. Warm tones for the flowers—oranges and apricots in orchids and calla lilies—raise the temperature still more.

Late afternoon in Udaipur, India

photograph Tricia Guild

Earth colors are naturally compatible with one another, but mixing the warm and cool tones can be difficult. It is often easier to interject a note of a different color altogether, such as clear blue, lime, or lilac, in a scheme using peat and cool browns and neutrals, than to add the orange that might initially seem a more natural choice. Take inspiration from the desert cultures of Rajasthan in India: against the scorched earth colors of the landscape, the vibrant lemon-yellow, brightest lime, shocking-pink, and blue costumes of the tribespeople almost stand out in 3D. These colors come from earth pigments, from the colored cones of dyes piled high in the markets, softened by washing and drying in the sun and wind. Perhaps this is the reason they sit so well with the drier, calmer colors of sand, stone, and soil.

When you are using warmer earth colors, the scheme may veer toward pink or orange—the cool pink of raw plaster or the clay colors of terracotta. Cool it down by introducing a little lime green or dove-gray—these colors are natural counterparts for chunky, rough-hewn wood and highly-textured fabrics. The cooler earth tones, such as peat-brown, birch, granite, and taupe, are perfect for modern interiors. They seem to translate well to large loft spaces with stone or pale wood floors, and look good with low-slung, horizontal styles of furniture, whether contemporary pieces or classics from the roll call of twentieth-century design. Keeping the scheme purely tonal is a good opportunity to play with pattern. Stripes of varying widths and textures can be countered by curvy furniture or the swaying stems of white flowers. Or make modern use of floral fabrics, mixing them with stripes and checks or hanging long banners like articulated shades at tall windows.

flat browns provide the base for a modern mix of stripes and pattern

Large pieces of furniture in charcoal-grays and chocolate-browns anchor the expanses of space in this airy loft apartment. Banners of floral fabric sound a softer,

almost Asian note at the windows; rather than shutting out the surrounding buildings, they frame fragments of views, the tones of brick and glass beyond,

adding a further layer of color and texture. Alone, dark stripes might appear too cool and masculine; mixing them with flowers is both sensuous and surprising.

natural colors and textures as a setting for low, sensuous shapes

The entirely natural color scheme in this London loft apartment is enriched by careful attention to shape and texture. The high ceilings are further heightened by the low, horizontal shapes of the furniture. The curves of the armchairs, rope seats, and oval table inject a softer, more sensuous note amid the angular lines, while the branching arms of the cactus and the copper floor lamp stand out like sculptures. The subtlest touches of color come into play in the banners of patterned fabric strung at intervals along the wall of windows, and in the geometric alcoves set into the walls, which serve as niches for ceramics and sculpture. The flowers pick up on these tones. Simply replacing these pale tones with stronger shades would give the room a totally different atmosphere.

The different natural materials that contribute to the color scheme of this room bring their own unique textures and associations. The coolness of aluminum, the pale stone floor, and the slab of slate that runs along the fireplace are countered by the warmer tones of copper and light wood and the rich chocolate-brown of wenge wood. The properties of black and brown are susceptible to changes of light and texture—dark velvet is sensuous and unexpected in such a space; gloss paint or enamel is smart and shiny, reflecting the light dramatically; ceramics have a seductive earthy sheen. Lots of white, in the details as well as on the walls, allows the room to breathe more freely: there is white in the stripes on curtains, cushions, and upholstery, as well as in the sculptural shapes of vases and ceramics.

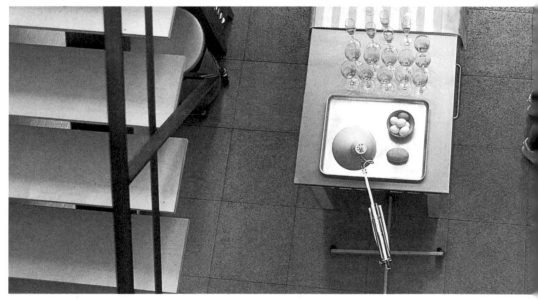

work in progress

pages 68-71

earth ocher terracotta

Pages 68-71 The warm wood tones of the floorboards were the starting point for a warm earth palette for this first room—I followed the tones of off-white to include the pink of raw plaster, peachy oranges, and pale browns and beige. The introduction of lime was crucial to inject some life into the scheme and prevent it from appearing cloying. Note that very little fabric—just the upholstery of the large wooden sofa and a few pillows—was needed to create this warm effect. Subtle paint colors such as buff and raw plaster would also look good as part of such a scheme.

Pages 76-80 The peat browns in this loft living room are very flat—at times you can hardly tell if they are brown or gray. This dark brown is a very neutral color and marries well with stripes, glass, metal, and the deep chocolate brown of wenge wood, as well as small areas of duck-egg blue. The angular, somewhat masculine effect of all these stripes is countered by a bold and original use of pattern, particularly at the windows: mix stripes with floral fabrics and more feminine, transparent fabrics for a subtly surprising look. The cooler naturals—taupe, dove gray and pebble—mix well with peat browns.

Pages 82-85 The pared-down, simple style of the next room as it appears from a distance, belies the rich pattern and detailed motifs on some of the fabrics: gold on chocolate brown, stripes that look handpainted, delicate plaid on moiré silk. The clean, low lines and simple shapes of the furniture allowed me to play with pattern without it appearing fussy. The cool charcoal-gray chenille on the sofa is countered by a bright acid lime stripe, while accents of cooler, paler color are added in the painted niches in the wall. The room sees an unusual but stunning alliance between raw natural earth colors and textures (unbleached linen, slubbed and striped, and fine-textured cream linen) with gold (gold-printed fabric borders, gold stamped motifs on wallpaper, gold plaid on silk). The effect is subtle and particularly sensitive to changes of light—the gold is set glowing by sunshine and candlelight.   TG

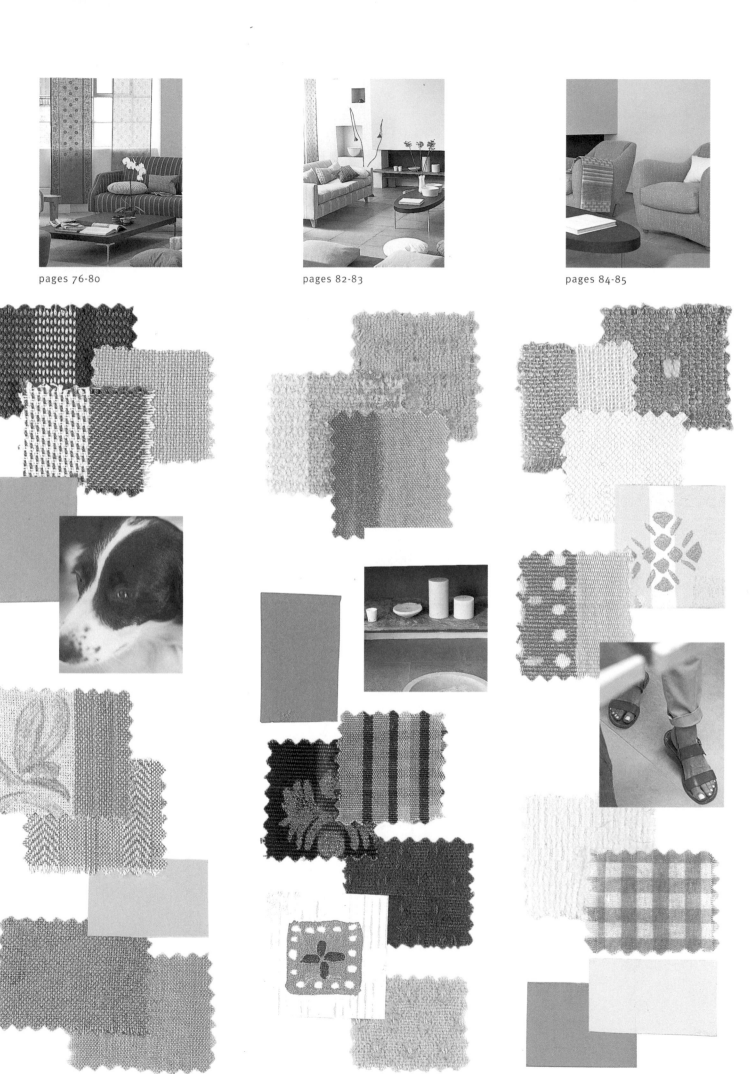

pages 76-80

pages 82-83

pages 84-85

for details of fabrics and paints used in the rooms on these pages see page 223

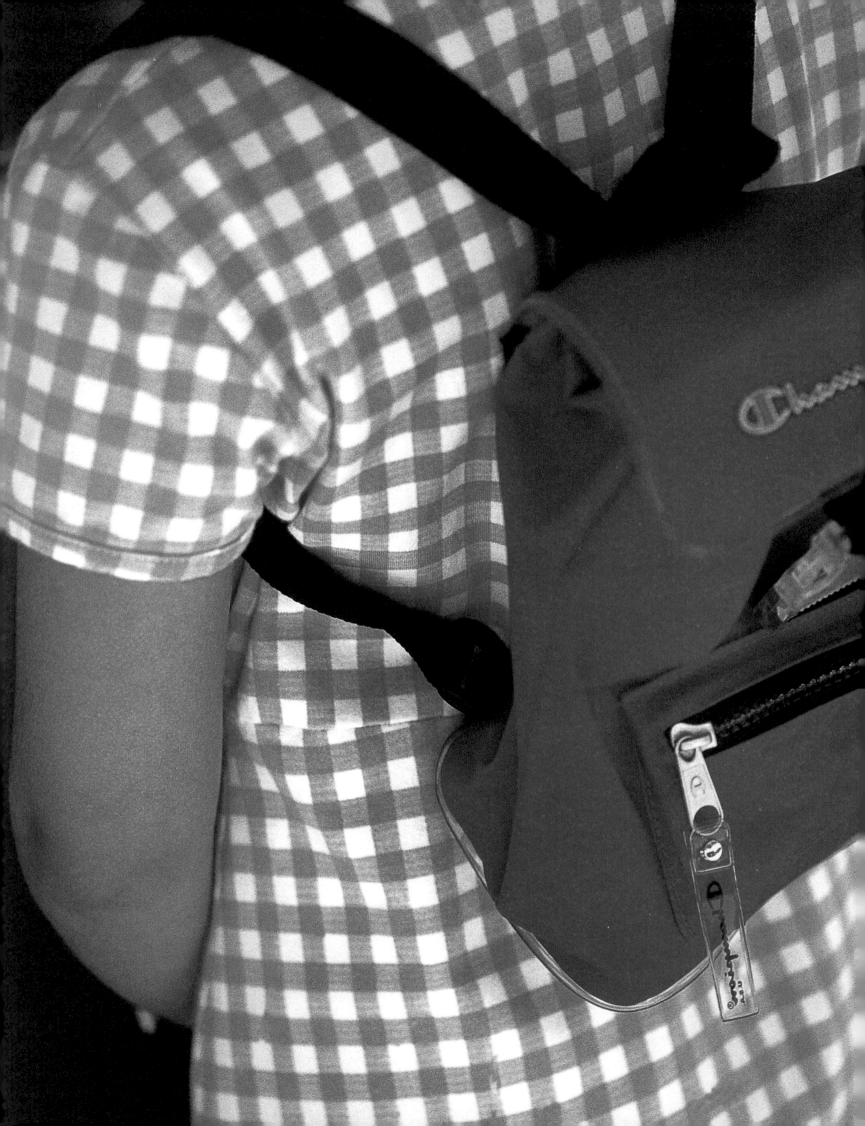

pink

karmin

rubin

rosso

magenta

rojo

crimson

amapola

cerise

poppy

red

rose

peony

scarlet

karmesin

rouge

pavot

rosa

pink

karmin

rubin

rosso

magenta

rojo

crimson

amapola

cerise

poppy

red

rose

peony

scarlet

karmesin

rouge

pavot

rosa

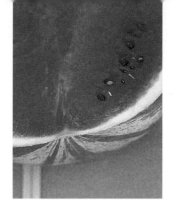

pink magenta red

Running all the way from the hotter oranges through deep reds, crimson, magenta, and fuchsia to pink, this is a dazzling, daring

group of colors, which should be used with care. Reds of all shades are startling, sensuous. Just a single red flower in a quiet

interior can have the impact of a sudden kiss. Without reds and pinks, life would somehow seem sad.

The eye is immediately drawn to red. Apparently, it is the color that requires the most adjustment in the muscles of the eye

in order to be seen, but we don't need scientists to tell us it is eye-catching. Think of how a figure dressed in red stands out against

a landscape, or how poppies seem to float in 3D before a field of grain. Throughout history and in all cultures, red has been used

where instant impact is vital—for road signs and traffic signals and warnings of danger. It signifies excitement, energy, arousal.

Red is the color of passion and romance: red hearts for valentines, red lights outside brothels; in China it is the color for luck

and marriage. All pinks are sexy and romantic, from the shocking pink of a Fifties Schiaparelli ball gown to the elegant charm of a pale

pink boudoir. Pink may be created by adding white (and maybe some blue) to red, but it is not just a paler shade of red. The two colors

are so distinct that they carry independent effects and associations. Magenta, fuchsia, and crimson, where red and pink meet, are deep,

color-saturated tones with a unique intensity of their own. They can all add a wonderful warmth and excitement to interiors.

the warmth of a single red wall creates instant impact

The impact of a single red wall in a room where almost everything else is neutral is quite simply stunning. This is not an overpowering shade of

red, and the texture is almost translucent, so you feel the warmth rather than the heat of the color. Framed by doors painted neutral slate-blue,

everything else in the room can be quiet and natural—pale wood, beige linen, white cushions and flowers—save for a couple of red cushions and

small hand-thrown pots. Using red is about balance: too much is uncomfortable and can sometimes feel overpowering; too little looks fussy. The

right amount, as here, can create a cozy backdrop to a wall of books—a warm place to curl up and read or dream.

Women in a carriage, Jaipur, India

photograph: Tricia Guild

pinks, oranges, and mauve—an unorthodox use of strong color and pattern

Persimmon, hot orange, raspberry pink, and grapey mauves—in a smaller room, and without balancing expanses of white, these hot colors might be

overwhelming. Instead, in this large, open space, there is a lightness of touch and texture that keeps the mood modern, airy, and exciting. The

shocking pinks and patterns of Indian saris were the inspiration for the paisley print banners that hang at the windows; the same colors are picked

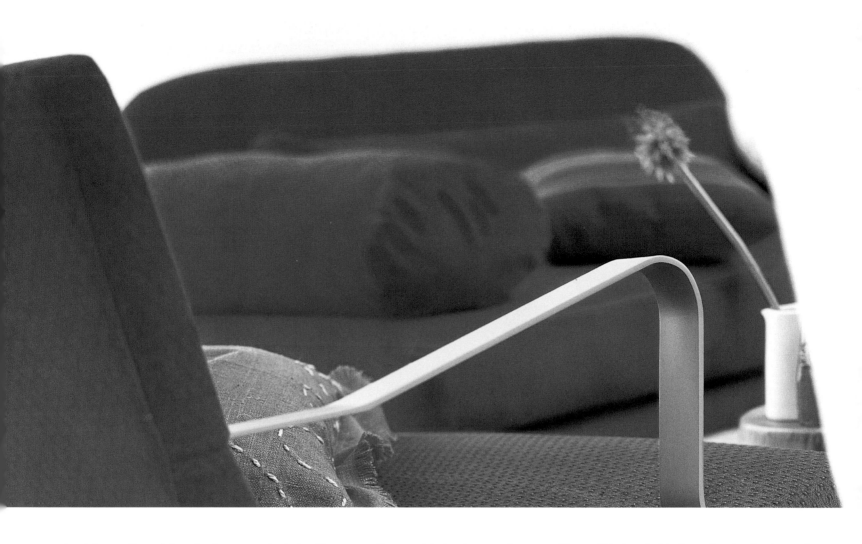

up in plain muslins, pink and crimson washed chenille, orange linen, red-hot pokers, and mauve alliums. This is a bold, dynamic mix of color and

pattern which breaks all the rules. Pale wood floors and furniture contribute to the calm, cooling neutral backdrop, while a grapey mauve, which

would appear warm in cool surroundings, instead reads as cool against these flowery firework colors.

Many people are afraid to use red; it might appear old-fashioned, or simply overpowering, or they fear that red will clash—with pinks, with oranges, with the wrong shades of purple or blue. But it's the rules, not the color, that are old-fashioned. To rule out decorating with reds is to miss out on all the warmth and dynamism of this group of colors. Reds are a fantastic asset to the contemporary interior, especially when used together. You just need to know how to use them.

A degree of discipline is necessary when using all colors, but especially with reds. One often feels the need to cool them down: to move toward the bluer end of the palette with fuchsia and magenta, or to counter them with cooler shades of blue, acid-green, or naturals. Texture plays a vital part, too: red velvet is soft and sensuous; in linen this color is crisply contemporary. Translate this same red to translucent silk or muslin at a window and it instantly becomes delicate. Small accents of red can appear like jewels, adding joy and richness to the plainest interior.

Look for the warm, subtle tones, where purple becomes magenta, or where shocking-pink slips over into mauve. Mix them with oranges and deep crimson reds—the effect is exciting, exotic, voluptuous. But remember: without white or naturals as part of the scheme, the impression could be uncomfortable or even oppressive. Red and white has a fairytale freshness about it—the Queen of Hearts, checked gingham, a pricked finger in the snow—while natural linen and cool unbleached muslin tones are quieter, more contemporary companions.

hot and cool contrasts create an extraordinary energy

The subtle use of cooling contrasts, such as lime-green and pale blue, is the key to success in this ambitious pink, red, and purple color scheme.

Without the lime doorway, embroidered curtains, and even the sprigs of alchemilla and other leaves, the impact of all these closely related tones

could be cloying. And yet it works—the pale pinks and powder-blues of the larger room continuing through to the smaller room, with its stronger

colors and backdrop of strong, shocking-pink on one wall. There are bold juxtapositions of color in both rooms—a broad crimson stripe on the nasturtium orange sofa, red cushions on mauve chairs, and, in the large room, a mixture of pinks, strong blues, and turquoise. Again, the grape tones have a cooling influence beside the hotter, stronger hues, and even the warm terracotta floors read as neutral in this context.

work in progress

pink magenta red

Pages 94-95 When using these daring hot colors, one needs to inject some coolness to prevent the effects from being overpowering. The delicious raspberry red of the wall in this study is countered by the pale wood floor (remember that the same wood tone could appear warm in a white or pale blue room), lots of white, and the flat zinc blue of the molding that frames the view from the living room. Using door frames of a flatter color such as slate blue, dove gray, or olive green to frame bright rooms is an idea worth experimenting with.

Pages 98-100 The use of large, splashy flower fabrics in the second room might be considered a daring and lively way to treat a loft space, but the large, open spaces give the huge floral prints room to breathe and set their painterly energy free. The fabrics bring together strong reds, greens, and shocking pinks—colors not often seen together. Plenty of balancing, textured white fabrics, as well as a floor of flat zinc blue, ensure that the scheme is a success—bold, fresh, and contemporary, rather than overpowering or muddled. Mixing bold patterns is easy if one keeps to a strict palette and includes enough whites and naturals.

Pages 102-3 The last two rooms here use virtually the same palette of hot, fruity reds, oranges, and purples in two very different spaces. In a London loft, the scheme revolves around the highly-patterned paisley print used at the windows; all the other colors in the room—the persimmon, tangerine, grape, raspberry, pale Parma violet, and lime—appear first on this fabric and crop up again in the chenille-upholstered chairs, the pillows and throws, and smaller details. It's the balancing neutrals that hold the scheme together—the pale wood floor, the pale lilac background of the curtain fabric, the off-white linen that offsets the mix of stripes and patterns.

Pages 108-10 In the Italian living room, I chose to respond to the period architecture with a more rigorously modern use of color—too much pattern here might have ended up looking fussy. Instead, you have the exciting contrast of the old beamed ceiling and doorway with a huge modern sofa upholstered in a bold, simple orange, red, and magenta stripe. And instead of going for neutral colors on the walls, one wall is a beautiful deep pink—an unusual, contemporary choice for a Tuscan house—while the doorway is outlined in lime green—affecting all the other colors and bringing the whole room right up to date.   TG

pages 98-100

pages 102-3

pages 108-10

for details of fabrics and paints used in the rooms on these pages see page 223

purpura susina

lavendel amethyst

glicine **violett**

avender malva lila

wisteria violet

lilac plum mauve

mallow lilla grape

lavande malva

purple raisin lilac

wisteria violet syren

violetta susina

mauve plum purple

glicine violett

avendel lilla grape

aisin amethyst

illa purpur mallow

rape malva lila

avender plum

lavendel amethyst

lavender malva lila

wisteria violet

lavande malva

wisteria violet syren

violetta susina

mauve plum purple

glicine violett

raisin amethyst

lilla purpur mallow

grape malva lila

lavender plum

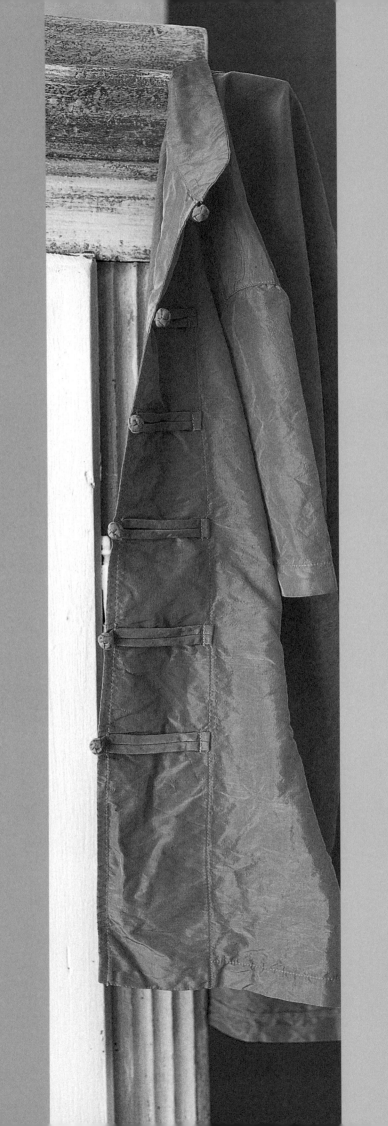

mauve lavender purple

Where does blue become mauve? Somewhere between delphinium and lavender, but just the other side of bluebell? Purple cuts a

rich swathe through the color spectrum, taking in all the shades from the palest mauve to the deepest, inkiest indigo. It embraces

cool tones, such as clear lilac, the bluer mauves, the gray-blue bloom on black grapes, as well as the warmer eggplants, deep wine-

reds, and the blackish-purple of the darkest sweet peas. The same shade of mauve can actually be hot or cold, depending on the

colors it is set against: grape and plum, for example, appear as warm accents in clear blue or aqua rooms, while among hot oranges,

reds, and pinks they will sound a cooler note.

Some mauves almost cross over into pink: there are mauves that border on magenta; crimsons with just too much blue to be

red. There is endless richness in this group of colors, whether used all together or juxtaposed with lime-greens or yellow. Some of

the most wonderful mauves are found in the flower world: in the pale pannicles of wisteria, transforming entire buildings during

May and June; in the two-tone blooms of lupins; in bearded irises, or the dark velvet faces of violets and pansies. Flowers also

provide inspiration for accompaniments to mauve: think of lavender flowers, with their cool, gray-green leaves, and translate this

combination into linen and silk; or the glowing orange stamens of the saffron crocus among its purple satin petals.

Artists have always been mesmerized by mauve. Monet used it in every shade when painting and repainting his water-lily

garden at Giverny; Bonnard also used mauve to capture the changing reflections of sunlight on water. But perhaps no artist has

explored the subtle, even spiritual qualities of purple as deeply as Mark Rothko, in the Rothko Chapel in Houston, Texas.

cool mauves and powder-blues in an airy attic bedroom

A cool lilac-mauve on the walls, powder-blue fabrics, and dove-gray painted floorboards create an air of freshness and stillness in this top-floor

guest bedroom. The colors all come from the cool end of the mauve palette. Stronger accents of blue appear in the turquoise ceramic fireplace and

embroidered bedcover, and in stripes on silk cushions with accents of lime. There is plenty of white—on the wall behind the bed, in white sheets,

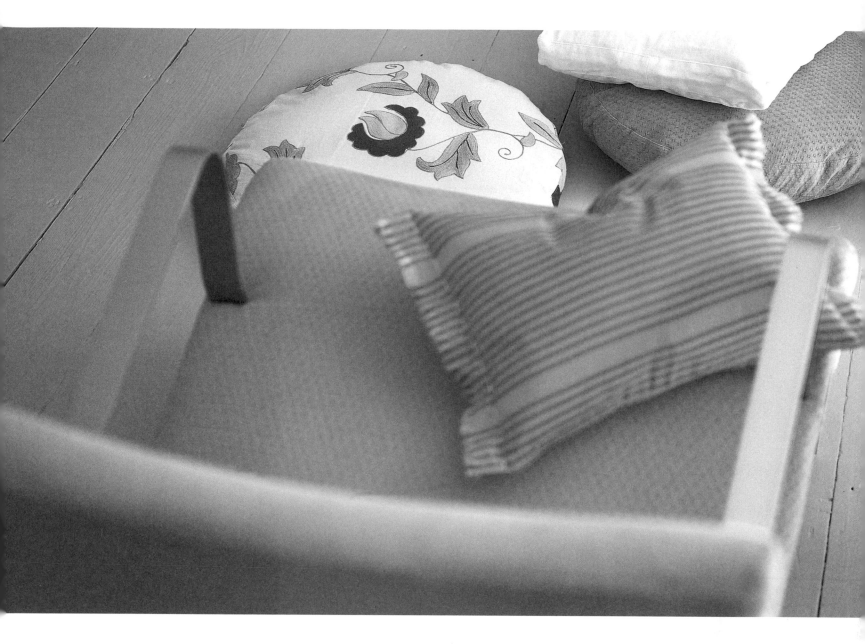

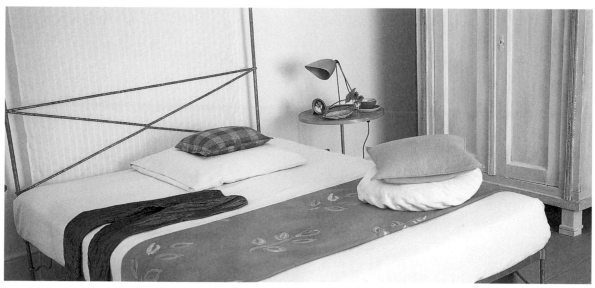

and in the wooden armoire, washed a chalky white but with some turquoise showing through—which keeps the scheme crisp rather than insipid and

pastel. Great care has been taken when choosing the furniture—graceful modern shapes and materials sustain a light, airy, and contemporary

atmosphere. The aluminum of the chair arms, bed frame, and table lamp play off the gray of the floor to become a silvery color within the scheme.

Dawn and twilight are the times of day when mauve moves in and steals the ground. In certain lights, pure white can take on mauve hues, gray shadows appear purple. Mauve is a remarkably subtle color, sensitive to tiny variations in light and texture. Imagine the impact of the same shade when seen and felt in silk, linen, matte paint, or clear plastic. There is a wealth of difference, in emotional resonance as well as aesthetics, between a warm woolen throw and rustling iridescent silk, the petals of a pansy and the glitter of an amethyst. These subtleties can be explored and exploited when using mauve in interiors.

Mauve's natural partners are its neighbors on the color wheel—blues of all shades, the darker crimson reds, and pinks. Use the colors all together for a rich, exotic atmosphere, adding more or less white to lighten or intensify the mood. Turquoise and aqua look good with warmer violets and mauves, while cooler tones look surprisingly good with dark chocolate-brown. Many shades of mauve are set off by a silvery grayish green, from lavender through clear lilac to deepest eggplant and grape.

The neutral base of mauve is a flat grayish grape color which can be mixed with almost anything—try wine-red or lime-green, or even matte olive. Grape, in all its tones, from warm plummy red to neutral, is wonderfully offset by small amounts of yellow.

For a cool color scheme, team a powdery pale mauve with powder-blue, pale gray, palest aqua, and plenty of white. This is a wonderfully calm collection of colors for a bedroom—you could add shocking pink cushions for a punch of pure color. For a warmer mood, combine almost any shade of mauve with crimson or magenta.

Wedding proce... ...ur, India

ph: Tricia Guild

an unusual use of mauve in a modern bathroom

Mauve adds just the right note in this simple yet luxurious modern bathroom. Translucent muslin shades throw a watery violet light around the whitewashed brick walls, and this quality is picked up in the choice of other colors and materials: the plastic lilac chair and chest of drawers. In such a pure and simple color scheme, the dark wood floor reads as a third color, adding natural depth and warmth.

lilacs, blues, and mauves bring light into an old country farmhouse

In this living room in Tuscany, warmer tones of mauve play against the pinkish-terracotta tiled floor. An armchair is upholstered in lilac, blue, and magenta

embroidered cotton; these colors resonate around the room in the stripes on a silk pillow, the padding of an ottoman, the gleam of a candlestick, a vase

of frilly sweet peas. A lightness in the shapes, tones, and textures sits well against the dark period fireplace and ancient wooden beams.

mauve lavender purple

pages 120-22

Pages 120-22 In this bedroom, I made the decision—that has the most delicate effect—to paint two tonally similar shades of mauve and blue on adjoining walls. The two shades—palest lilac and a bluebell blue that is almost mauve—look beautiful together and help to give the room its air of heavenly calm. On the floor is another pale color from the same tonal range—the softest dove gray. In the furnishings we went for a few strong violets and mauves, the strong turquoise of the fireplace, and touches of lime green to anchor the palette and prevent it from seeming insipid. The other two walls are painted white, and there is lots of white and off-white fabric on the bed and furniture.

Pages 124-26 The second room has an almost Asian feeling about it, brought out by the way the muted color palette comes through the natural linen—flat grapey grays and pale lavenders that work particularly well with natural linen colors, pale mushroom and gray. The use of delicate pattern complements these elusive colors—loose, painterly florals and small motifs stamped in gold. The range of colors is kept to a minimum; the room feels calm and restful. This is a good palette for a bedroom.

Pages 130-32 The next bedroom becomes a bold modern take on the boudoir, with big, splashy, handpainted cabbage roses taking the place of tiny rosebuds. It's still a feminine space, but bold and exciting. The color palette is taken from the rose print: clear cobalt blue, violet, pale lilac, magenta, and pink. The other bold flower print on a white ground helps to balance all the saturated color, as do pillows and bedlinen in off-white linen. It is fun to mix bold florals with other prints and checks; the colors of the rose print are picked out in the pink silk check.

Pages 136-37 In this Italian living room the palette is dictated by the crewelwork on the armchair. The jewel-bright colors are perfectly offset by the dull, unbleached muslin ground. On pure white or cream the effect would have been quite different; lighter but less surprising. The rich colors of the fabric—lilac, peacock blue, and deep crimson against the natural beige—are what give this room its individuality. The other colors, such as the harmonious combinations of blues and mauves on stripes and raised damask patterns, all relate back to it, creating a reassuring sense of unity. TG

pages 124-26

pages 130-32

pages 136-37

for details of fabrics and paints used in the rooms on these pages see page 224

aquamarine

aquamarine

aquamarine

aquamarine

aquamarine

aquamarine

aquamarine

aquamarine

aquamarine

aquamarine

aquamarine

aquamarine

aquamarine

aquamarine

aquamarine

aquamarine

turquoise aqua

Aqua, or aquamarine, is a wonderful, watery color, as alluring as it is elusive. Think of the color cast by an electric light shining up through a swimming pool at night; of the Mediterranean Sea, its sandy bottom visible on a clear summer's day; of a girl's eyes that vacillate between green and blue. Some of the most beautiful colors are almost undefinable, occupying the ground where two related colors meet and merge. Blues that are nearly greens, greens that slip imperceptibly toward blue—these are the colors that make up this section. Even their names are mysterious: turquoise, celadon, tourmaline; they are often the words for things associated with the color—sea-green, eau-de-nil, pistachio, robin's-egg blue. The range is wide, from the pale tints of ancient glass to the strong blue-green often seen in Federal-period houses. The defining factor is that it makes you wonder: Is that blue or is it green?

There are no flowers of this color except the startling turquoise Himalayan poppy, *Meconopsis baileyi*. Aqua occurs in nature in the glassy gems of the mineral world, in the gray-green leaves of artichokes, often tinged with purple, and in the countless blue-greens of the ocean. If blue is the color of the sky, aqua is that of water—it radiates the peaceful, calming qualities of a still sea. Perhaps because of its cooling, calming effects, aqua is often used in hot countries. In Tunisia and Morocco the interiors of houses are painted in aqua and turquoise; railroad waiting rooms in India are often a clear pale blue-green. Aqua provides a good ground for the hotter oranges, pinks, and reds also prevalent in these cultures; the exotic contrasts sing out in paintings by Matisse and Paul Klee. Somehow, though, the artist one associates most with this color is Cézanne—his red and russet apples against a cool aqua ground, the shimmering haze of sky, clouds, and leaves around his beloved Mont Saint Victoire.

contemporary aqua blues meet ancient wood and terracotta

In this impressive hallway, the thick stone walls have been painted a chalky, textured shade of aqua, which creates an intriguing contrast with the

warmer tones of terracotta tiles and old dark wood. Keeping the scheme purely tonal creates a romantic, yet somehow modern, mood. The seats

and backs of old Spanish cinema seats are painted rich turquoise, and there are modern ceramics of the same shade on the table and on the floor.

In keeping with Tuscan tradition, the borders around the base of the walls have been hand-painted in other colors: a soft lime-green and faded olive on

the risers to the stairs. This space works as a welcoming entrance hall, but when the candelabra is lit and the table set, it is swiftly transformed into a

romantic dining room.

unexpected pattern and bold modern contrasts

Pattern defines the space in this enormous open-plan apartment. To create a private sleeping area, a floating wall on wheels has been drawn up beside

the bed, one side patterned, the other side solid-colored. The use of aqua further divides this area from the rest of the loft, creating a calming, restful

space. Fabric banners with a bold blue tulip print hang like shutters at the windows; there are accents of different blues and aquas in the pillows and on

the chair. The scheme is totally flexible: a backdrop of pure white walls, painted floorboards, and plain bed linen ensures that in a few minutes, with a

different color on the screen and new fabric at the windows, one could create a space that would not only look but also feel quite different.

blocks and accents of strong turquoise applied like brushstrokes in an abstract painting

Careful use of color can have a unifying effect on potentially overwhelming spaces. In this double-height loft, different shades and textures of strong aqua

and turquoise have created an air of intimacy while losing none of the spatial drama. Translucent muslin shutters in indigo and aquamarine filter the

sunlight and send it in soft shafts across the room. The strong colors and rich materials—turquoise crushed linen, striped and gilded silk, sheer muslin,

peeling painted wood—are played against lots of balancing naturals in the whitewashed walls, bleached cotton, and warm wood floor. Contrasting accents

of deep pink, mauve, and lime bring warmth and harmony to the whole; a magenta peony in the foreground makes the blues appear even richer.

Calm yet compelling, bold yet strangely subtle, aqua colors sit happily side by side. The arc of the spectrum from violet to blue to aquamarine to green blends effortlessly both in nature, where the sea meets the sky or where green hills blur into blue-gray hills on the horizon, and in interior design. Aqua's natural partners are blues and greens from the same group, or colors just on either side (purple, lime-green), or complementary mixes like hot orange or a deep berry pink. With white, aqua has an almost clinical freshness; with cream it is tinged with nostalgia, like a 1930s' tearoom. With black it is sharp and dashing—a shiny Fifties' radio or the chromed fin of a car; with grape or taupe it is cool and contemporary.

There is something wonderful about using all the blues and greens together—they create a unique atmosphere, both peaceful and surprising. Take the aquas as far as green on the one side and to blue on the other, or even over into mauve, and enjoy the way the colors ebb and flow into one another at the extremes. Without white and naturals it can seem like living underwater.

White works well with aqua, both in large modern spaces and in small period rooms, but it needs other colors to be seen at its best. All cool colors work well with accents of warm contrast: a pinky-mauve throw on a pale aqua sofa, a painting with deep red or crimson tones. Or you can keep things slightly cooler with cushions of clear lilac silk. Play games with texture: cool tones in soft, warm fabrics have an intriguing allure—aqua velvet is virtually a contradiction in terms.

Two walls of this room are a strong textured turquoise with pigment swirled into the plaster; they are toned down by a chalky aqua blue on the dividing doors and quiet warmer accents of mauve and grape. Because all the colors are tonally very similar they work well together, creating a calm yet rich blend of tones and textures.

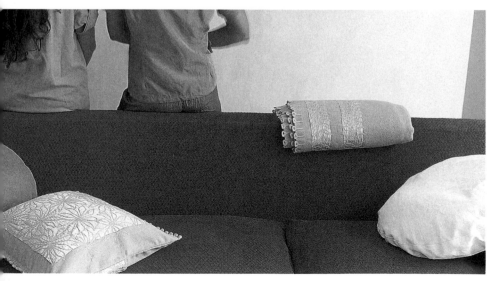

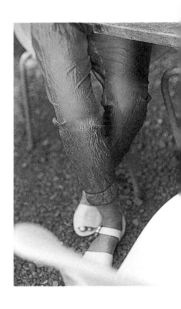

The exposed bleached oak floorboards increase the feeling of openness and space, the pale yet warm tones working as a complementary neutral color, along with the other wood furniture. There is also, as so often, a lot of white. White cushions and flowers splash white on a colored canvas. Creating a room is like painting: you add and subtract color until the result feels right.

work in progress

turquoise aqua

pages 148-49

Pages 148-49 People have come to expect lofts to be all semi-industrial materials and raw brick, when, in fact, it is often more exciting to use pattern—in a modern way, of course. Here, a refreshing, totally modern sleeping space has been carved out by the mixture of aqua floral fabrics on the articulated shades at the window and on the freestanding wall on wheels beside the bed. Using the same color range in two different-sized patterns and with other stripes and textures in the pillows on the bed works very well. Balancing it with lots of white creates an atmosphere that is fresh and dynamic, yet still condusive to sleep. White and aqua are always a successful combination—here the bold use of pattern is countered by large expanses of unadulterated white: on the bedlinen, the walls, and, most notably, on the gloss-painted floorboards.

Pages 150-54 The color of the floor is one of the most important single influences on the atmosphere of a room. A white floor, particularly a reflective white floor, profoundly affects the light and energy in the space and makes any color sing out in relief against it. Wooden floors have a warmer, rather more earthy feel, as can be seen in the second apartment, where a similar palette of aqua colors is seen in a rather different context. Here, smaller areas of white, on the pillows and other small items, help to provide the balancing neutrals, while a single crimson bloom appears like the splash of an artist's brush.

Pages 156-58 In the pale aqua bedroom the color is extremely soft, with walls painted palest powder blue and fabrics that are off-whites and very diluted shades of blue and green—there is an air of ambiguity as colors seem to merge into one another. The striped fabric brings the blues and greens together; the atmosphere created by these subtle colors is very simple, plain, and soft—ideal for a bedroom. Bright turquoise ceramics in the foreground prevent the whole scheme from slipping under water.

Pages 160-63 This double living room illustrates a richly satisfying partnership of cool aqua and warm berry and grape shades. One wall is a richer turquoise, the dividing doors are aqua-green; the upholstery is in shades of violet, lilac, mauve, and pale blue, with plenty of balancing white on walls, ceramics, and plain linen cushions. This is a confident, sensuous combination of colors—the different shades seem to blossom in each other's presence. TG

pages 150-54

pages 156-58

pages 160-63

for details of fabrics and paints used in the rooms on these pages see page 224

emerald lime grass apple viridian vert

peppermint menthe green sage apple

green eau de nil fern grün verde lichen

mint emerald manzana moss olive me

feuille pomme verdigris græs leaf grün

emeraude fern mela apfel herbe seawe

verdigris oliva jade limone sage emera

emerald lime grass apple viridian vert

peppermint menthe green sage apple

green eau de nil fern grün verde lichen

mint emerald manzana moss olive me

euille pomme veridigris grass leaf grün

emeraude fern mela apfel herbe seaw

veridigris oliva jade limone sage emer

emerald jade green

There are thousands of different shades of green. The palest, like the soft milky green of new cheese rind or the crisp translucency of a young pale white wine, are scarcely there at all—just a hint of something fresh and vital. The sharp citrus shades are harder to ignore: tangy limes and acid-greens that have the same refreshing, revitalizing effect on the eye that they would on the taste buds. There's the glamorous, glittering green of emeralds; the cool glassy mystery of jade. Other greens are more subtle: the deeper, duller gray-green of sedge and olive or that darkest bottle-green, almost black, found on many French front doors. Each has a different effect on the eye, the imagination, and the feelings.

The many different names we have for green testify to its obvious associations with nature: pea, leaf, fir, grass, apple, lime,

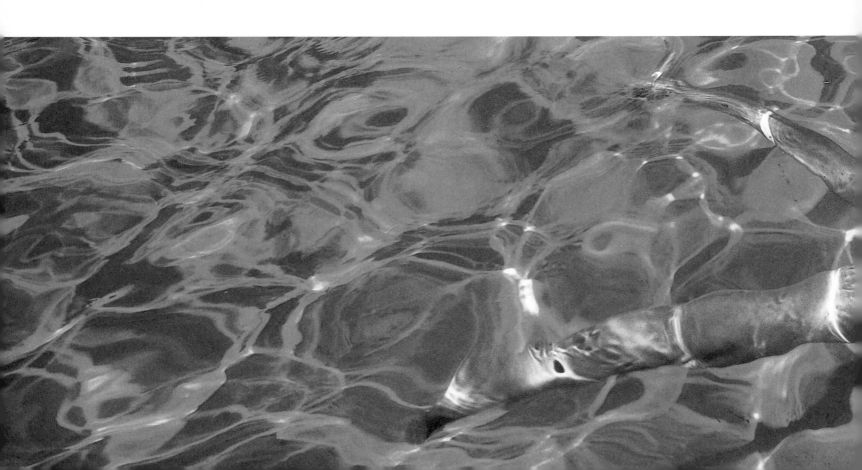

mint. You only have to think of a country lane in May to know that different greens mix effortlessly in the natural world. Its other common combinations are with white, brown, shades of mauve, and red, its direct opposite on the color wheel.

Over the centuries, the use of green around the home has sometimes been limited by certain prejudices and preconceptions: that it is unlucky, that it is too cool a color, even the old chestnut that "blue and green should never be seen without a color in between." Forget about old ideas, and develop your own, instinctive, emotional approach to color. Take time to look, long and hard, at two or three shades of green and notice their effects on you. Different greens can be clean, calming, intriguing, or exciting to different people and at different times. In color there are no constants; no rules that can't be broken.

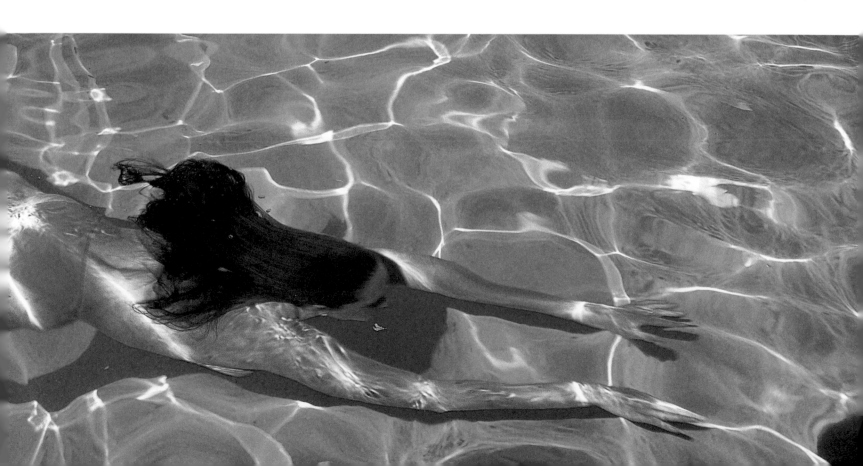

where aqua becomes green: fresh quiet tones for a bedroom

On the top floor of this spacious London house, the hallway opens onto this blue-green bedroom, a clear, calm, quiet room with accents of lime-green. The walls are painted freehand with stripes of aqua and lime; it is this, combined with the linen fabrics on the bed, that gives an overall impression of green rather than blue.

Calming neutrals allow the quiet freshness of this color combination to make a subtle impact: the soft dove-gray of the door and paler gray-painted

floorboards. The pale metal furniture becomes a silvery gray; wardrobes, cabinets, and tables are simply washed white. The effect is in the balance:

imagine the difference that the addition of a single crimson flower or shocking-pink silk pillows would make.

Lime-green and aqua are natural companions with a similar tonal effect. The bannisters that coil up the center of this house were once orange; painting them aqua creates a quieter, yet still energizing, contrast against the textured lime wall of the entrance hall. The dynamic freshness of lime works well with pale stone, wood, and concrete, and responds well to dramatic changes in light; it is a young, springlike color, with the power to raise the spirits.

Woman walking, Fatehpur Sikri, India

photograph: Tricia Guild

Green is a calm color. It is restful on the eye, which may be the reason it is commonly used in studies and libraries. But it is also the color of life, of rising sap and fresh new growth, and so can also have an uplifting effect on our spirits—particularly that sharp acid green of the first leaves of spring.

Green in the garden is the anchoring ground, the backdrop for blooms in jewel-bright hues. In interiors, it works well with accents of bright orange, mauve, or red, its complementary opposite on the color wheel. These brighter colors should be scattered like little surprises to highlight, rather than fight with, the green: a cushion here, a candle there, a splash in an abstract painting on the wall. When using pattern, big, bold modern florals look good in red and green—use them in large expanses at the windows or thrown across a bed or sofa. Lime-green can be used to bring a bright spark of life to brown or dark natural interiors, or to bring out the richness in different blues or purples. Lilac and lime is a fresh and dynamic combination, seen in arrangements of scabious with alchemilla leaves and on Indian women's saris.

Green needs plenty of balancing white to breathe. The stronger and richer the green, the more space it needs around it. Pure white works well with all greens, creating an atmosphere that is fresh, yet quiet—perfect for bedrooms. In rooms that have a view onto trees or a garden, green can permeate the interior from outside, bringing its own energy and an intriguing effect on the light. In Bonnard's famous paintings of nineteenth-century interiors, the dappled, dancing quality of the light suggests sun shining through a veil of gently moving foliage. By hanging translucent flowered fabric in banners at the windows you can achieve a similar effect.

shades of lime and orange glow in their true intensity against a backdrop of white

Bright colors clustered in one area can help define the space as one moves around a modern, open-plan apartment. The background colors in this loft are pale and neutral: a grayish wall, bleached boards, expanses of white on walls and ceilings. The strong lettuce-green of a large modern sofa is what carves the living room area out of the surrounding space: one area of vibrant color can have a dramatic impact. Accents of tangy orange are used sparingly on cushions and a silk throw. Don't be tempted to overdo the dots of color; with strong tones such as these, the contrast of pure white brought in again for cushions and ceramics is much more effective than another color.

palest lime, glassy reflections in a tranquil space

Pale green can be the subtlest color. In this unusual loft space, greens just this side of yellow and delicate pale mauves are reflected in the watery

surface of a wall of translucent glass. The pale tones and textures create a calm that is almost Zen-like. Low contemporary wooden furniture and

floral fabrics that have a hand-painted quality contribute to the quiet, almost Asian impression of this room.

emerald jade green

pages 172-75

Pages 172-75 Touches of pale pink work wonderfully with pale lime—it is another springtime combination, like blossom on trees, very fresh and unexpected. Put your hand over the throw on the bed and see how the color scheme would subtly change without any pink. The pink is what makes it so unusual, and what seems to make the lime green look even fresher and more vital.

Pages 176-78 Here, the palette is confined to green—a slightly yellower, pure lime which is as refreshing as a crisp apple. Green and white are a fresh, simple partnership which looks particularly good in this room, with all the different greens of the garden outside. Against this natural green backdrop, spontaneous splashes of color are provided from time to time by plates of fruit and vegetables in season, bright napkins, and dishes on the table. The expanses of green on the walls could be softened by the use of a patterned wallpaper.

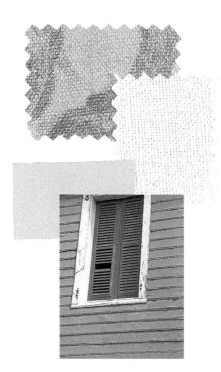

Pages 182-86 In this large loft it is orange that adds the contrast—green and orange, being opposite each other on the color wheel, create a particularly dynamic effect together. The huge green sofa is what marks out the seating area in this open-plan space—just a few smaller areas of contrast are all that is necessary to create a feeling of interest and comfort. One wall is green, and the rest are a cool ice-blue; there is plenty of contrasting white—cushions in contrasting citrus shades would have been too much in this space.

Pages 188-89 A stunning combination of delicate pale greens with soft lilac and gray-mauves is perfect for a bedroom or any other room where you might want to create a calm but romantic atmosphere. A mixture of small, delicate florals and patterns in soft feminine colors is a real tour de force, including in the palette softer, silvery shades of gray and natural stone color as well as white. The green used here is slightly bluer than the limes in the other rooms—softer and less yellow, which makes it a natural partner for the washed-out mauves and lilacs. The textures of natural linens are perfect for these colors—and a subtle herringbone weave sets off the florals in a cool, contemporary manner.   TG

pages 176-78

pages 182-86

pages 188-89

for details of fabrics and paints used in the rooms on these pages see page 225

amarillo
yellow
citrus
jaune
limone
saffron
cm
giallo
sonne
lemon

amarillo

yellow

citrus

jaune

bronze

saffron

giallo

lemon

yellow lemon citrus

Citrus, pale primrose yellow, lime—these are the colors of spring: the milky green buds of hyacinths nudging through the soil; the

sharp acid-green of new beech leaves, hanging like tatters of bright silk on branches with sunlight shining through them. After the

gray of winter, these colors have an uplifting effect on the human psyche when we see them in nature; the subconscious thrill is still

there when we use them indoors. A room furnished solely in lime, acid-yellow, and masses of white has a fresh, optimistic, spring-

like feel. Strong yellows can be hard to use, too hot and too heavy; but even these can be cooled and softened by a little lime-green.

Take inspiration from nature: daffodils are at their most beautiful when still in loose greenish bud; the yellow of their open trumpets

can seem just too strong. In addition to the obvious buttery and Chinese yellows, explore the more interesting natural tones around

the edges of the color group: creamy primrose, pale lemon, mustard, ocher, the neither-green-nor-yellow of some ripe pears.

Chartreuse, that wonderful greenish-yellow of absinthe and of alchemilla and euphorbia flowers, moves in and out of fashion, but it is one of the most fascinating colors of all. Adopted by the Aesthetic Movement in the late nineteenth century and satirized by Gilbert & Sullivan as "greenery-yallery," it has caught the imagination of painters and fashion designers ever since. Howard Hodgkin and Patrick Heron, two of our greatest colorists, make strong use of this color, while Romeo Gigli and Miuccia Prada have fashioned it into clothes of softest velvet and iridescent silk. True chartreuse, which has much more yellow and very little blue, sets off colors at the opposite end of the color spectrum: dark blood-reds through crimson and cranberry to grape. The slightly bluer shades look best with lavender, violet, and indigo. Think of a garden: the lime-yellow foliage of the honey locust tree as a leafy backdrop, with lilac-blue clematis, deep blue cornflowers, and smoky-red valerian weaving through them.

sunshine and citrus shades in a modern mews house

The cool angular lines of this modern mews house come alive with a stunning mix of citrus colors. The yellow and orange are surprisingly hot, but the

introduction of lime-green and a softer acid-yellow prevents them from seeming heavy. Skylit glass ceilings let the ever-changing light play across planes

of color on walls and stairwells. Looking down through the glass and metal gallery toward the kitchen, the yellow of the cabinet doors is muted by the

cool neutral tones of zinc and indigo-gray. Against any other color the plastic chair would probably read as gray.

Yellow is not always an easy color to use, and the hotter and harder the yellow the more difficult it is. The key to using these colors is delicacy. You have to get the balance right. The addition of white is crucial to avoid an overripe, claustrophobic feeling. Think of the sun shining through silver birch trees, with budding daffodils beneath. Keep it light, bright, and spring-like.

Perhaps because of the connotations of sunlight seen through young leaves, citrus colors have an affinity with translucent materials. Layers of muslin in lemon and lime, hung like banners at windows, will bathe a room in these delicate colors. Yellow is traditionally used in rooms that catch the early morning sun, but a zingy acid-lemon will bring the feel of sunshine even to north-facing rooms. When using strong, rich yellows, avoid treating all the walls: these colors look best as blocks or accents. At the palest end of this section, cream, when used against white, becomes a color in itself: the very palest yellow, between off-white and primrose. Cream paint, pale wood, the natural textures of unbleached muslin and linen have a subtle, sensuous beauty, either alone or as a ground for indigo or blue.

Try using all the citrus shades together, with pure white, like fresh air, filling the space between; the effect can be wonderful. Contrasting accents of bright pink, pale mauve, wine-red, and aqua can be added with restraint; for inspiration, look at the yellow stamens of flowers against their jewel-bright petals. Grayish blues and cool browns are other natural companions, but avoid warm browns with hot yellows unless you want to evoke the Seventies.

the colors of spring light up a large white space

Fine, checked voiles and opaque plastic flirt with the translucent quality of citrus colors and, with the ever-changing light, add to the many nuances

of yellow and lime already chosen for the room. These are colors that can be used together in many different, closely related shades. A backdrop of

white allows their natural brightness to shine through—the neutral tones of taupe, stone, and untreated string add rawness and depth.

lime-green brings a contemporary buzz to an Italian country kitchen

Lime enlivens this country kitchen, bringing the colors of warm spring sunshine to a room that is welcoming and always full of friends. Acid-green

combines well with cooler, flatter colors, such as the slate blue of the shelves and cabinet doors and the flat olive-green in traditional stripes and

stencils around the walls. A painted cabinet with one lime door, one white, and a slash of tomato-red across the top arrests the eye in one corner.

In front of it, a scrolling antique metal candelabra appears both modern and sculptural.

a softer use of citrus in a period Swedish bedroom

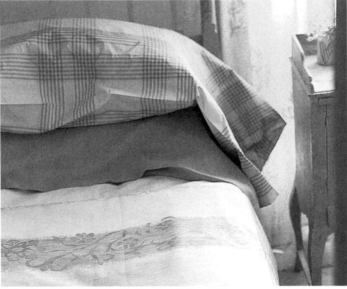

Softer citrus shades, tempered by warmer naturals such as natural linen and pale wooden boards, bring a fresh, modern feel to this bedroom in an eighteenth-century house in Sweden. Muted shades of white, cream, pale lemon, cool yellow, and lime are coupled with the soft sensuous textures of silk and muslin, washed velvet, crumpled linen; the effect is calmer than the sharper citrus shades and more suited to a bedroom. Gold stenciling on the curtains supplies a romantic, rather feminine feel; the mixture of stripes, checks, and other patterns evokes Swedish traditions, while simultaneously appearing fresh and modern.

work in progress

pages 198-201

yellow lemon citrus

Pages 198-201 Red, lime, and citrus yellow are an arresting combination in this modern mews house. There is just enough green in this yellow to prevent it from seeming heavy and cloying—instead, it is the perfect foil for the rich turquoises, blues, and tangy oranges that appear elsewhere in the room. Bold colors often look good alongside other bold colors, and are brought more alive by the strong natural light in this skylit space. Hot orange and yellow have been used to paint the large expanses of wall in the stairwell—the blue flowers add a necessary note of coolness to the scheme and pick up on the colors in the flowered fabric.

Pages 202-4 The coolest shade of yellow has been used for this bedroom, with touches of green on the bedcover and accents of apple green all around. The walls are white with a pale citrus yellow on the lower section; the space is framed by a turquoise door frame that brings out the delicacy in the scheme. This is a small room, but the fresh color scheme prevents it from ever seeming nostalgic.

Pages 206-10 This loft is an example of how the color of the floor can change everything. If this floor was not painted white, the fresh, almost springlike atmosphere would be somehow diluted; the colors would not sing out in their true intensity and might even be drowned by too dark a shade of wood, for example. The use of citrus colors at the window creates a dappled light not totally dissimilar to sunshine shining through new leaves—perfect for spring.

Pages 214-15 The Swedish bedroom uses the warmest yellow in our palette with lots of balancing neutrals—ecru, white, and white-painted furniture. Even a dark room such as this can seem sunny and warm when the right shade of yellow can be found; the layering of lots of delicate yellow-patterned shawls, throws, and cushions create an airiness and welcome calm, while touches of gold and coffee suggest excitement. The overall impression is of warmth and contentment.   TG

pages 202-4

pages 206-10

pages 214-15

for details of fabrics and paints used in the rooms on these pages see page 225

Women in Jodhpur, India

photograph: Tricia Guild

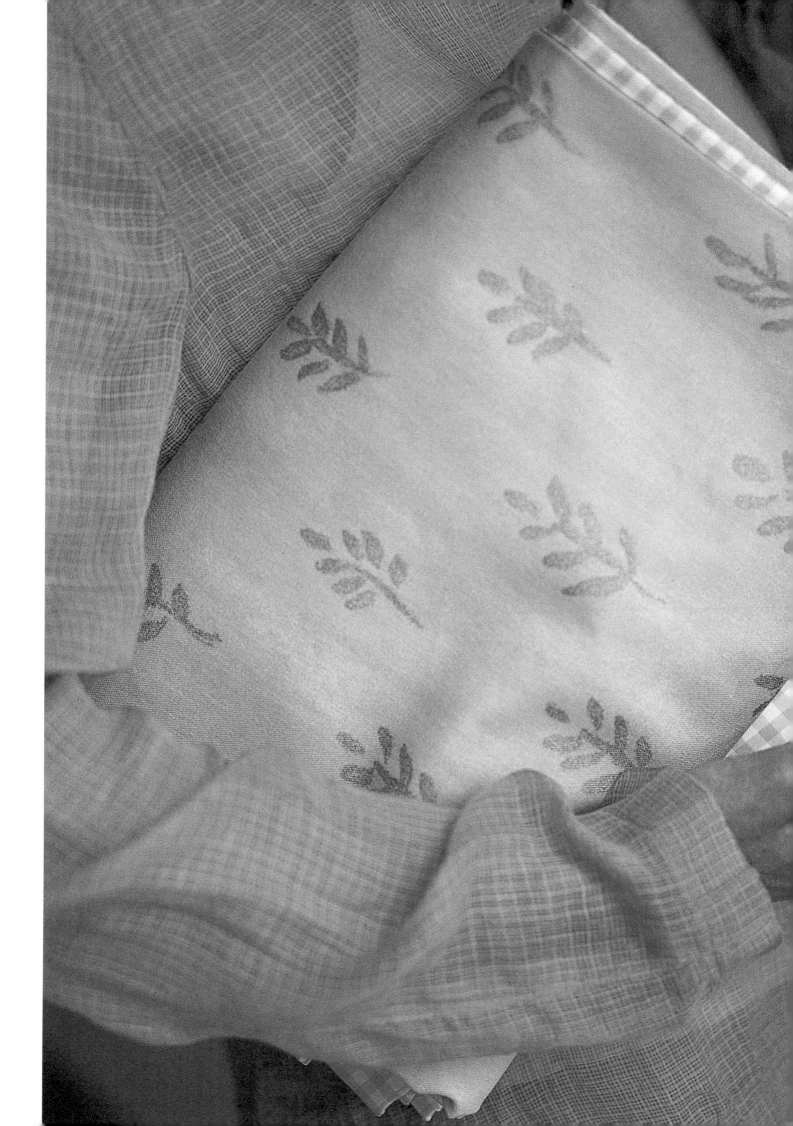

fabric, wallpaper, and paint directory

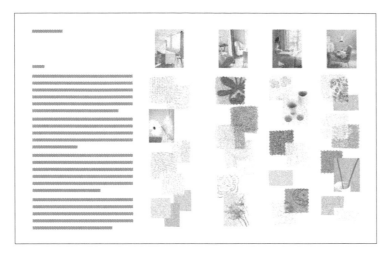

pages 34-35

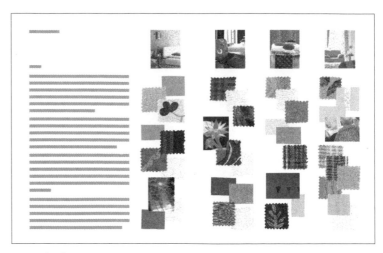

pages 60-61

white ecru natural

Pages 16-19

Roscrea (white) F621/02

Brera (white) F562/15

Adyar (natural) wallpaper P294/05

Kilfinny (white) F491/01

Rovigo (chalk) F671/25

Birch paint

Hemp paint

Ice Blue paint

Pages 20-23

Navan (sand) F653/01

Kilrea (natural) F617/01

Arklow (natural) F623/01

Callan (white) F619/02

Chalk paint

Quanjin (ivory) wallpaper P302/01

Pages 26-27

Sakura (buttermilk) wallpaper

   P305/03

Kilcoran (natural) F861/01

Kilcoran (white) F861/02

Almond paint

Ajisai (celadon) F847/02

Rathmullan (white) F865/02

Pages 32-33

Shallu (Delft) F876/01

Morning Sky paint

Mallow (white) F860/02

Mokku (china) F869/01

Rovigo (ice blue) F671/23

Cloud paint

Ice Blue paint

blue indigo ice blue

Pages 42-45

Cirrus paint

Brera (chalk lilac) F562/19

Jalaja (oyster blue) F673/02

New Mauve paint

Chennai (mauve) F594/04

Minakari (blue) F674/03

Mallow (white) F860/02

Brera (white) F562/15

Jodhpur Blue paint

Pages 52-57

Maddur (lilac) F589/02

Brera (white) F562/15

Dahlia (cobalt) F791/02

Kaani (blue) F675/02

Solferino (white) F690/11

Cornflower paint

Hiyoku (hyacinth) wallpaper

   P244/11

Nalanda (magenta) F656/04

Callan (white) F619/02

Pages 46-48

Chanderi (aquamarine) F822/03

Brera (white) F562/15

Mandriola (petrol) F844/07

Cloud paint

Deep Water Blue paint

Tabriz (brown) F832/05

Pebble paint

Kesari (cobalt) F829/03

Pages 58-59

Amru (slate) F830/04

Tasi (celadon) wallpaper P293/08

Pale Jade paint

Tafta (natural) F836/07

Shiraz (brown) F835/06

Rovigo (ice blue) F671/23

Chennai (pale blue) F594/06

Adyar (turquoise) wallpaper

   P294/04

Rovigo (chalk) F671/25

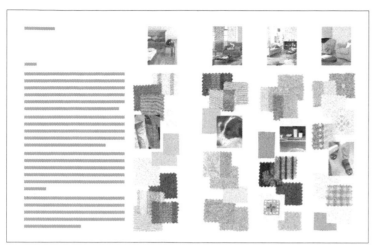

pages 86-87

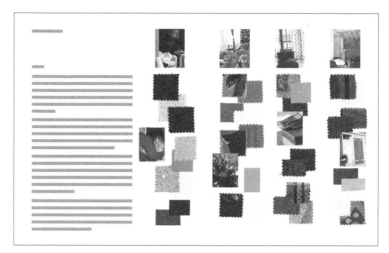

pages 112-13

earth ocher terracotta

pink magenta red

fabric, wallpaper, and paint directory

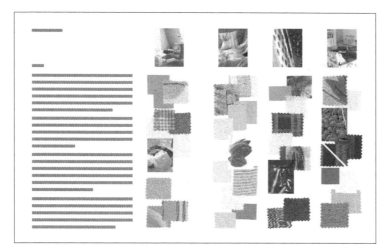

pages 138-39

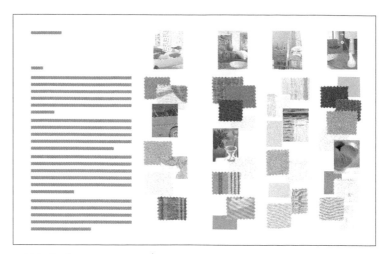

pages 164-65

mauve lavender purple

Pages 120-22

New Mauve Paint

Kaani (oyster) F675/01

Lavender paint

Alipur (lavender) F658/08

Rovigo (lilac) F671/12

Brera (white) F562/15

Callan (white) F619/02

Cold White paint

Rovigo (ice blue) F671/23

Chennai (pale blue) F594/06

Bhatu (turquoise) F638/04

Pages 124-26

Glin (natural) F859/01

Uchiwa (slate) F852/01

Paglia (heather) wallpaper P255/09

Heather paint

Quanjin (chalk blue) wallpaper P302/08

Salvia paint

Brera (chalk lilac) F562/19

Brera (white) F562/15

Grape paint   Lilac paint

Pages 130-32

Damascena (cobalt) wallpaper

P280/02

New Mauve paint

Callan (white) F619/02

Maddur (lilac) F589/02

Brera (white) F562/15

Dahlia Voile (lilac) F808/03

Brera (hyacinth) F562/03

Rajkot (magenta) F661/06

Pages 136-37

Kaani (natural/mauve) F675/05

Brera (white) F562/15

Trivandrum (mauve) F664/02

Chennai (mauve) F594/04

Viola paint

Cold White paint

Brera (chalk lilac) F562/19

Solferino (lilac) F690/05

turquoise aqua

Pages 148-49

Brera (turquoise) F562/13

Mei P'ing (turquoise) F484/03

Rovigo (ice blue) F671/23

Capucine (ivory) wallpaper P276/05

Brera (white) F562/15

Akru (lavender) F834/08

Chalk white paint

Pages 150-54

Nalanda (cobalt) F656/02

Brera (hyacinth) F562/03

Brera (turquoise) F562/13

Dove paint

Brera (white) F562/15

Quilon (turquoise) F622/04

Bhatu (turquoise) F638/04

Indian Ocean paint

Pages 156-58

Rajshani (pale blue) F640/01

Patadar (china) wallpaper P262/01

Ice Blue paint

Pontaccio (delft) F561/04

Callan (white) F619/02

Celadon paint

Chamba (green) F660/03

Brera (pale aqua) F562/20

Pages 160-63

Sea Green paint

Rovigo (grape) F671/11

Rovigo (lilac) F671/12

Rovigo (ice blue) F671/23

Brera (white) F562/15

Kalamkari (turquoise) wallpaper

P202/18

Killalla (white) F497/01

Brera (chalk lilac) F562/19

Patadar (azure) wallpaper P262/02

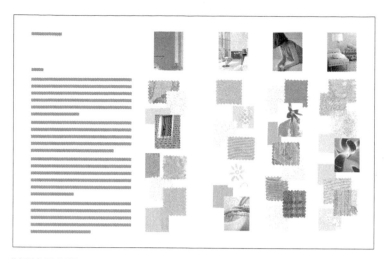

pages 190-91

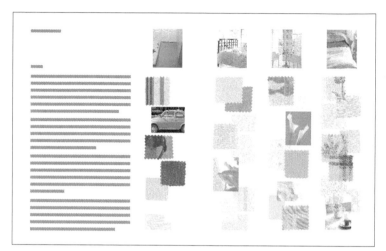

pages 216-17

emerald jade green

yellow lemon citrus

Designers Guild stockists

Designers Guild lifestyle is available from the Designers Guild store at 267-277 Kings Road, London SW3 5EN

Designers Guild Fabrics and Wallpapers are distributed in the US and Canada by:

Osborne & Little Inc
90 Commerce Road
Stamford
CT 06902 USA
203 359 1500

ATLANTA

Ainsworth Noah & Associates
351 Peachtree Hills Avenue
Suite 518
GA 30305
404 231 8787

BOSTON

Shecter Martin
One Design Center Place
Suite 111
MA 02210
617 951 2526

CHICAGO

Osborne & Little Inc
Merchandise Mart
Suite 610
IL 60654
312 467 0913

DALLAS

Boyd Levinson & Company
1400-C HiLine Drive
TX 75207
214 698 0226

DENVER

Shanahan Collection
Denver Design Center
595 S Broadway
Suite 100-S
CO 80209
303 778 7088

FLORIDA

Design West Inc
1855 Griffin Road
Suite A-474
Dania
FL 33004
954 925 8225

HOUSTON

Boyd Levinson & Company
5120 Woodway - Suite 4001
TX 77056
713 623 2344

LOS ANGELES

Oakmont
Pacific Design Center
Suite B647
8687 Melrose Avenue
CA 90069
310 659 1423

METRO NEW YORK

David Parrett
14 East Lane
Madison,
NJ 07940
201 635 5545

MINNEAPOLIS

Gene Smiley Showroom
International Market Square
275 Market Street
Suite 321
MN 55405
612 332 0402

NEW YORK

Osborne & Little Inc
979 Third Avenue
Suite 520
NY 10022
212 751 3333

PHILADELPHIA

JW Showroom Inc
The Marketplace
Suite 304
2400 Market Street
PA 19103
215 561 2270

PHOENIX

Swilley-Francoeur & Hunter
2712 North 68th Street
Suite #4000
Scottsdale, AZ 85257
602 990 1745

PORTLAND

Stephen E Earls Showrooms
208 NW 21st Avenue
Suite 200
OR 97209
503 227 0541

SAN FRANCISCO

Randolph & Hein
Galleria Design Center
Suite 101
101 Henry Adams Street
CA 94103
415 864 3550

SEATTLE

Stephen E Earls Showrooms
520 South Findlay Street
WA 98108
206 767 7220

WASHINGTON DC

Osborne & Little Inc
300 D Street SW
Suite 435
WDC 20024
202 554 8800

TORONTO

Primavera
160 Pears Avenue
Suite 210
M5R 1T2
CANADA
416 921 3334

Designers Guild products are available in over 40 countries including the following :

ARGENTINA

Mrs Miranda Green
Cabello 3919
1425 Buenos Aires
00 54 1 802 0850

ARUBA

Terra Nostra Decorations NV
Caya GF Croes 2
PO Box 5080
Oranjestad
00 297 8 30312

AUSTRALIA

Wardlaw Pty Ltd
230-232 Auburn Road
Hawthorn
Melbourne
Victoria 3122
00 61 3 9819 4233

AUSTRIA

Victoria Schoeller-Szüts
Boersegasse 9 #10
A-1010 Wien
00 43 1 535 3075

BELGIUM & LUXEMBOURG

Acanthus Interiors Sprl
J. Eerdekenstraat 27
B-3001 Heverlee
00 322 2 503 4787

BERMUDA

Howe Enterprising !
PO Box HM 3222
Hamilton HMPX
00 1 441 292 1433

BRAZIL

Humberto
Escritoria Central
São Paulo
R. Barata Ribeiro 263
00 55 11 257 3977

CHILE

Les Tissus
Nueva Costanera 3730
Vitacura
Santiago
00 56 2 246 5665

COLOMBIA

Denise Webb & Associates
Dise-o Interior
Calle 79B # 7-59
Int.4A
Bogotá
Colombia
00 571 255 6194

CURAÇAO

The Jungle
Lindberghweg #1
00 59 9 9 465 8640

CYPRUS

L. I. Christofides
P O Box 1310, 9
Loukis Akritas Avenue
Nicosia
00 357 2 772 939

FRANCE

Designers Guild Sarl
10 rue Saint Nicolas
75012 Paris
00 331 44 67 80 70

GERMANY

DESIGNERS GUILD
EINRICHTUINGS
GMBH
DREIMUHLENSTRASSE 38A
80469 MÜNCHEN
00 49 89 23 11 620

GREECE

PERSEFONE N
DIAMANDAS & CO EE
49 ANAGNOSTOPOULOU
STREET
GR-106 73 ATHENS
00 30 1 361 3810

HONG KONG

AVANT GARDE
DESIGNS LTD
SHOP 133 THE MALL
PACIFIC PLACE 2
88 QUEENSWAY
00 852 2 840 1627

ICELAND

VEFUR
25 SKOLAVORDUSTIG
101 REYKJAVIK
00 354 552 2980

INDONESIA

PT CIPTA MERKURIUS
INTERNATIONAL
JALAN ABDUL MUIS
NO 24-26
JARKARTA PUSAT 10160
00 62 21 381 0968

ISRAEL

SEZAM LTD
255 DIZENGOFF STREET
SHOP 406
63117 TEL-AVIV
00 972 3 609 4471

ITALY

DESIGNERS GUILD
SRL
VIA MASONE 2
24121 BERGAMO
00 39 0 35 222 800

JAPAN

MITSUI & CO LTD
2-1 OHTEMACHI
1-CHOME, CHIYODA-KU
TOKYO 100
00 81 3 3285 1111

KOREA

SOUTH SPRING
INTERNATIONAL CO
LTD
YOUNG DONG
PO BOX 344
SEOUL 135-603
00 82 2 549 6701

KUWAIT

AL SEDRAH
ESTABLISHMENT
PO BOX 2685
HAWALLI 32027
00 965 265 4083

LEBANON

PERSPECTIVES SAL
PO BOX 4198, BEIRUT
00 961 1334 120

MALAYSIA

RUFFLES
FURNISHING
c/o SINNAN F17/18
1ST FLOOR
PLAZA YOW CHUAN
JALAN TUN RAZAK
50400 KUALA LUMPUR
00 60 3 242 8573

MEXICO

ARTELL SA DE CV
CALLE 20 NO 9
COLONIA SAN PEDRO
DE LOS PINOS
MEXICO 03800 DF
00 52 5 272 2861

NETHERLANDS

WILHELMINE VAN
AERSSEN AGENTUREN
PRINSENEILAND 7-9
1013 LL
AMSTERDAM
00 31 20 626 6474

NEW ZEALAND

WARDLAW (NZ) LTD
PO BOX 9451
NEWMARKET
AUCKLAND
00 64 9 520 3000

PERU

ROMANTEX SA
AV. PAZ SOLDAN 185
SAN ISIDRO
LIMA 27
00 511 441 3339

PHILIPPINES

JODY'S FABRICS INC
2ND FLOOR LAPUZ
BUILDING
19 PASAY ROAD, MAKATI
METRO MANILA
00 63 2 843 5832

POLAND

ROZNE ROSNOSKI S.C.
UL OLEANDROW 5
00929 WARSAW
00 48 22 8253582

PORTUGAL

PEDROSO E
OSORIO
RUA FERNAO LOPES
409-2
4100 OPORTO
00 351 2 617 1497

SAUDI ARABIA

AHMED G ALESAYI
PO BOX 5651
JEDDAH 21432
00 966 2 669 0071

SINGAPORE

LINEA TRE
402 ORCHARD ROAD
4-02/05 DELFI
ORCHARD
SINGAPORE 0923
00 65 734 5540

SOUTH AFRICA

H F HOME FABRICS
LTD
60 OLD PRETORIA ROAD
HALFWAY HOUSE
MIDRAND
1685 JOHANNESBURG
00 27 11 805 0335

SPAIN

USERA USERA
AYALA 56
28001 MADRID
00 34 9 1 577 94 61

SWEDEN

TAPI
KOMMENDÖRSGATAN 22
114 48 STOCKHOLM
00 46 8 661 0380

TAIWAN

GRC DEVELOPMENT
COMPANY
1F NO.15
LANE 53
HSIN YI ROAD
SEC 4
TAIPEI
00 886 22 752 9740

THAILAND

SHEET'N SHADE
CO LTD
344 RAMA 3 ROAD
BANGKLO
BANGKORLAEM
BANGKOK 10120
00 66 2 289 4655-6

TURKEY

DIZAYN TEKSTIL
DIS TIK LTD
TESVIKIYE ATIYE
SK:7/4
AK AP 8200 SISLI
ISTANBUL
00 902 12 247 3206

UNITED ARAB EMIRATES

DG HOME
FURNISHINGS UAE
CITY TOWER 1
SUITE 304
PO BOX 1178
DUBAI
00 971 4 314 324

UNITED KINGDOM

DESIGNERS GUILD
267-277 KINGS
ROAD
LONDON SW3 5EN
0044 171 351 5775

for further
information
please contact

DESIGNERS GUILD,
3 OLAF STREET,
LONDON
W11 4BE
0044 171 243 7300
0044 171 243 7333

Email:
info@designersguild.com

Website:
www.designersguild.com

© DESIGNERS GUILD TM
IS A REGISTERED
TRADEMARK

acknowledgments

My special thanks to our brilliant team who have worked together so closely on this book—James Merrell, Elspeth Thompson, Meryl Lloyd, Jo Willer, and Anne Furniss. Thanks to a great team at Designers Guild for all their support and commitment, and also much appreciation to the following people who have participated so enthusiastically: Clare Brett, Drew Butler, Julian Cloke, Tom Corey, Paul and Janet Czainski, Lucy Dickson, Andy Gashe, Lisa Guild, Michael Heindorff, Harry Henry, Liz Hodges, Anjeli Kapur, Ralph Levy, Adam Marsh, Arne Maynard, De Metz Architects, Gilly Murphy, Russell Norman, Richard Polo, Mark Poswillow, Claudia Rose, Mark Naughton-Rumbo, Estelle Shores, Lucy Stentiford, Conroy Winter, Caroline Wiseman.

Published by Clarkson N. Potter, Inc., 201 East 50th Street, New York, New York 10022. Member of the Crown Publishing Group.
Originally published in Great Britain by Quadrille Publishing Ltd. in 1999
Random House, Inc. New York, Toronto, London, Sydney, Auckland.
www.randomhouse.com
CLARKSON POTTER, POTTER, and colophon are trademarks of Random House, Inc.
© Photographs James Merrell 1999
© Text Elspeth Thompson 1999
© Design and layout Quadrille Publishing Ltd 1999
Printed in Germany

Library of Congress Cataloging-in-Publication Data
Guild, Tricia.
White hot: cool colors for modern living/Tricia Guild; photographs by James Merrell; text by Elspeth Thompson with Tricia Guild.—1st ed.
   p. cm.
   Includes index.
   1. Color in interior decoration. 2. Colors—Psychological aspects. I. Thompson, Elspeth. II. Title.
   NK2115.5.C6 G87 1999
   747.94—dc21   99.32987
                                                                       CIP

ISBN 0-609-60493-7

10 9 8 7 6 5 4 3 2 1
First Edition